DELHI Heritage TOP 10

Baolis

DELHI Heritage TOP 10

Baolis

VIKRAMJIT SINGH ROOPRAI

Foreword by Sohail Hashmi

NIYOGI BOOKS

Published by
NIYOGI BOOKS
Block D, Building No. 77,
Okhla Industrial Area, Phase-I,
New Delhi-110 020, INDIA
Tel: 91-11-26816301, 26818960
Email: niyogibooks@gmail.com
Website: www.niyogibooksindia.com

Drawings and illustrations by Nupur Bhatnagar
Cover illustration by Gurdev Singh

Editor: Sukanya Sur
Design: Shraboni Roy

ISBN: 978-93-89136-11-1
Publication: 2019
Reprint: 2023

Printed at Niyogi Offset Pvt. Ltd., New Delhi, India

CONTENTS

FOREWORD

All ancient civilizations, those that graduated from hunting and gathering to settled agriculture, had developed methods of harnessing water for agriculture and for daily consumption. Each civilization adapted to the peculiarities of their climatic conditions, the terrain they inhabited, the seasonality of precipitation, and developed techniques that were best suited to their conditions.

In different parts of the world from the heights of Andes where the Incas lived to southern Mexico, Guatemala, Northern Belize, and Western Honduras inhabited by the Mayas, from the flood-prone plains of the Nile in Egypt to the lands inhabited by the Assyrians, the Sumerians, the Romans, the Chinese, and other ancient civilizations, there were as many solutions to problems of seasonal plenty and scarcity, even excess and flooding, or paucity and absence of water that were unique to each society.

In India, during the times about which we do not know enough, there were those who settled in the

Indus Valley and whose settlements gradually grew into towns and cities. It were these people who developed a network of drains, some open while some underground, to carry water to all parts of the city. They also built large public baths, and we are still trying to understand how the entire system worked.

The inheritors of these great cultures keep talking about their rich ancient civilizations, and how advanced were their techniques of urban planning, and it is the same with us. Whenever we participate in international colloquia on hydrology and on water management, we never tire of preening ourselves before the world community, telling them about the underground network of drains and the great baths and the hydrants, the remains of which can be seen even now. We try to present these as unique, and this we do because we have convinced ourselves that we are the fountainhead of all knowledge. It does not occur to us that each great civilization, some as old as ours, and a few even older, had found their own methods of solving the most crucial problem of human existence—water management.

Boasting about a past—partly understood, partly misunderstood, and mostly imagined—is the foundation upon which the edifice of the nation state is constructed. Despite the phenomenal diversity—climatic, cultural, social, and historical—that has informed these myriad ideas of a glorious past, there is one similarity that cuts across all, and that is our refusal to learn anything from this fantastic past, especially when it comes to practices that help sustainable living.

We are creating newer and newer methods to exhaust our resources, ones that we do not have the mechanisms to regenerate. And one of these resources is water. The speed with which we are consuming, polluting, wasting, and destroying this one resource that every civilization had learnt to conserve makes one wonder if we can actually claim to be more civilized than all earlier civilizations.

The slim volume *Delhi Heritage—Top 10 Baoli*s put together by Vikramjit Singh Rooprai, a young heritage enthusiast and photographer, looks at stepwells and their importance in meeting the water requirements of the residents of the capitals that rose and fell in what is now the national capital territory of Delhi, and also of the villages that have existed in this region much before the capitals came up.

Aside from the stepwells, the residents of Delhi depended on natural waterbodies, man-made ponds and reservoirs, wells, natural streams, and canals, one of which brought water to the city of Shah Jahan across a distance of 130 kilometres. Most of the natural and man-made waterbodies have been encroached upon and built over, while the others are counting their last days. The canals are mostly gone, as are most of the wells. What remains of the traditional waterbodies are a score or so of stepwells, some visible and still in use, while others marking their time before they too meet the fate that has befallen most traditional waterbodies.

You will find interesting details about the positioning of the stepwells, their location and their links with places of worship; you will come across little nuggets of information about architectural details and also imagined and created histories based on folk recounting; but, most importantly, you will come across a deep and abiding concern for our shared heritage and ideas that can perhaps help us arrest the ever-depleting water table of Delhi.

According to figures presented by the Central Ground Water Board before the Supreme Court of India on

8 May 2018 (*TOI*, 9 May 2018), the water table in almost all of Delhi, except for a few pockets of west and central Delhi, is in a semi-critical or critical zone.

The ever-declining water table of Delhi owes much to the large number of cars that need more and more land under roads. So we have a situation where, for every sq. km of land in Delhi, there are 224.7 kms of roads [1,483 sq. kms (total land area in Delhi) - 3,31,198 kms (total road length in Delhi)]. Add to this the tendency to concretize all walkways and all courtyards, which are then decorated with potted plants. There is little chance for rainwater to seep into the ground, and then we have the builder lobby constantly pumping out water for their multi-storey towers.

Vikramjit's proposal to use the stepwells as aquifers and to divert rainwater run-off into them might be one way of, at least, partially reversing the unending cycle of continuous exploitation of our most precious exhaustible resource—water.

Sohail Hashmi

PREFACE

The idea of writing about *baoli*s came to my mind sometime around 2012. Since then, I started exploring and learning more about these structures. It took me five years to collect the information that could do justice to such a book.

To my surprise, many travellers writing in English ignored the water structures of the towns in their accounts. Most writers took the water structures for granted, probably because they were available in such abundance. Except for one or two major *baoli*s, most historians did not mention the others. On the face of such a situation, this book became a challenge. I had to learn Urdu to study documents that have not been translated yet. A book in Japanese and few records in Persian revealed many secrets, after I got some help in deciphering them. Some historic records mention more than hundred *baoli*s in Delhi, out of which less than fifteen are accessible to the public today. After many debates and lengthy discussions with experts, I was able to compile this book.

While selecting the *baoli*s for this book, I investigated major factors like accessibility to visitors, cleanliness of the water, cleanliness of the surroundings, usage, size, shape, and the age of the structures. The factor that surprised me was the size. I calculated the area covered by each *baoli* on the surface, and while I was hoping for Ugrasen ki Baoli to be the largest in Delhi, as it appeared to be the longest on the map, the circular *baoli* of Kotla Feroz Shah won the race. Rajon ki Baoli followed it, pushing the longest *baoli* to the third rank in terms of area. Given that the research took almost half a decade, before I could start writing, I was witness to several changes that happened around these *baoli*s. But this made my job more difficult, as the water level and the surroundings kept changing every season, and the order of my list was affected with each rainfall. Few *baoli*s got restored during this period, completely changing the way they looked. The order of *baoli*s in this book is based on the data available in November 2018.

On 24 October 2009, I visited Rajon ki Baoli, the first *baoli* in my life. That time, the water level in the *baoli* was so low that if I had dipped my hand right in the middle of the tank, my wrist would have remained dry. A decade later, we could only see two out of the four storeys of this *baoli*, as water had filled more than half of the structure. In 2010 and 2011, I paid many visits to Rajon, Gandhak, and Ugrasen *baolis*. These three happened to be most famous back then, apart from Hazrat Nizam-ud-Din ki Baoli. On 31 May 2012, I was invited by Sohail Hashmi to accompany him and Dr Narayani Gupta to see the Red Fort Baoli. I had not heard about this one till then. This visit was a game-changer, as, for the very first time, I saw a functioning *baoli*. The water pockets around the well were much higher than the water level due to which spouts of water were gushing down the well. The water level inside the well and the tank was low, since water was pumped out of the *baoli* for irrigation purpose. I always had a perception that *baolis* were long, rectangular structures. The Red Fort Baoli, being an L-shaped structure, broke that myth. Later, my expeditions led me to find that the *baolis* of Feroz Shah Kotla, Arab ki Sarai, and Tughlaqabad also don't follow a rectangular pattern.

INTRODUCTION TO *BAOLIS*

What is a *Baoli*?

Since the beginning of civilization, humans have tried to hold water for their consumption. In India, techniques to store and source water have evolved from the Great Bath of Mohenjodaro to modern dams and reservoirs. In the last 1,500 years, people in South Asia have refined their ways of accessing subterranean water by extending the utility of wells. We started by digging wells, building step ponds and baths, and later realized that water used for bathing and drinking was no longer potable. Hence, the architects came up with an interesting solution in some parts of the subcontinent, where wells and tanks were constructed separately yet connected by a window. These structures became popular by many names like *bawadi, bavari, vaav, pushkarni, barav, baoli, bavali, bain*, or simply 'stepwell' in English.

Facing page: The Red Fort Baoli tank, with the well shaft visible in the left and steps from the west visible partially in the lower right corner

Speaking of Delhi, a typical *baoli* consists of a well which is attached to a separate water tank or basin. Wells are dug deep enough to penetrate the underground confining the impervious layer (crossing the underground water table/unconfined aquifer). Tanks are built at a much lesser depth with a window between the well and the tank. They may or may not connect with the first layer of underground water aquifer. The window allows water to get transferred from the well to the tank. Since the tank has a larger surface area, it exerts less pressure on the water surface. On the other hand, the well is a long cylindrical shaft exerting higher pressure on the water, thus transferring water from the well to the tank, but not vice versa. Medieval builders believed that since the water from the tank can never return to the well, the tank water can be used for bathing, washing, and other chores without the risk of it contaminating the water in the well, thus making the well water safe for drinking. A flight of stairs is constructed to reach the tank. Multiple levels are raised as the tank gets deeper, each with an optional set of chambers. These chambers serve a dual purpose: *first*, to provide strength to the structure by counterbalancing the inward thrust at the sidewalls, and *second*, to provide room for its visitors. It should be noted that several architects experimented with new, innovative styles

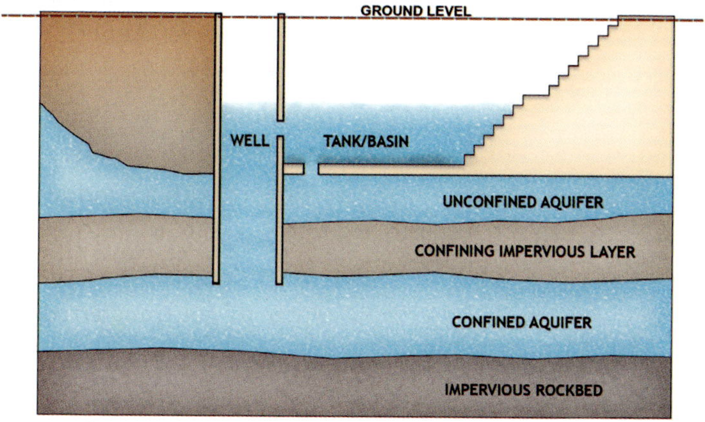

Diagram of a *baoli* with steps, a tank/basin, and well, positioned over the underground water aquifers

and gave us such fine architecture like the Red Fort's L-shaped *baoli* and Feroz Shah Kotla's circular *baoli*.

Another interesting thing to note is that many *baoli*s in Delhi have their wells towards the south with steps leading from the north to the south. In case of the *baoli*s of Hindu Rao Hospital Complex, Tughlaqabad, and Arab ki Sarai, the well and tank arrangement does not match the said description, but one flight of steps in each case still descend from the north to the south. Old Fort Baoli and Ugrasen ki Baoli had a different requirement and space constraint, hence the steps lead from south to the north. The only exception here is the *baoli* of Feroz Shah Kotla, which is circular in shape.

A possible explanation for such an architectural alignment is the effect of sunlight. If the deeper portion (that is, the tank) is towards the north/south, it is exposed to sunlight for the least amount of time. This keeps the water cool and provides shade to those who climb down a large flight of steps to reach the water. The north-south alignment also ensures that for half a day, one side remains in the shade and the other side gets proper sunlight. Sides switch as the sun moves. It benefits during both summer and winter.

*Baoli*s and wells work on the simple process of sedimentation. While the well penetrates the confined aquifer, the walls of the well/*baoli*/tank also allow the seepage of water through small gaps between the stones. This creates water pockets behind each such gap. The pockets are interconnected by tiny water channels created naturally after rainwater seeps in through the catchment area. Mud, mixed in water, settles in the tank, and one gets clean water on the top.

*Baoli*s were not just sources of water, but also served as important community sites. Almost all *baoli*s and tanks had a place of worship attached to them. The oldest reference in Delhi is of Anangtal in Sanjay Van, Mehrauli. It is a stone's throw away from the temple of Yogmaya. The Surajkund tank (in Faridabad) came later, built by Raja Surajpal Singh Tomar. It had a Sun Temple attached to it. The Muslim reign began after this, following which almost every *baoli* constructed was either attached to a dargah or a mosque. Every religious place needed water for its daily rituals and for the visitors. And so, they always had a source of water within the complex. Depending on the footfall, it could be a well, a tank, or a *baoli*. It is very difficult to say whether the *baoli*/tank/well was built because of the religious structure or otherwise. One very interesting practice related to public waterbodies can still be seen in the smaller villages of India. According to this practice, men do not go to any public waterbody around noon. Noontimes were always (and still are) reserved for women. If men need water, they walk close enough to the waterbody such that they would not be able to see anyone present there but can talk to someone inside. They either cough or shout to check if women are present at the waterbody. In case there are ladies using the *baoli* or the pond, they respond and give the man some water. If no response comes, the man is free to go to the water source. I do not think that such a practice is followed at the wells. But I have observed this custom in many villages of Punjab and Uttar Pradesh in the last fifteen years.

People also avoid touching the base of the tank while using buckets or when diving, as it disturbs the settled mud and the water will have to be left idle for some time before it can be reused.

REVIVAL OF *BAOLIS*

Can the *baoli*s be revived? This is a common question I often encounter. Can these *baoli*s solve the water problem of Delhi? Can we connect the *baoli*s, wells, and other historic waterbodies with our modern water circulation system?

The answers to such questions may sound easy, but would be as difficult to implement. Currently, water from only four *baoli*s is being pumped out, namely the Red Fort, Old Fort, Feroz Shah Kotla, and Banjaron ki Baoli. *Baoli*s like Gandhak ki Baoli, Rajon ki Baoli, and the ones inside the dargahs of Hazrat Nizam-ud-Din and Khwaja Kaki contain water, but have not been used. Stagnant water becomes dirty and may lead to diseases and infections. Since the *baoli*s of Nizam-ud-Din Dargah and Gandhak are believed to be holy and medicinal, people take a dip in them and sip the water as a religious practice, despite the hygiene factor. The underground water connected to these *baoli*s must also be contaminated. To completely revive the *baoli*s, it is important that we dry them up, clean the bed, and direct rainwater to them for a few seasons. We will also have to ensure that this redirected water is circulated properly, so that all the choked pores in the walls of the *baoli*s are desilted. And while we do all this, another challenge standing our way is the sewerage system in Delhi. The sewerage in this city is quite old and, at certain places, the underground sewers are punctured. This also contaminates the groundwater. Even if we manage to clean the *baoli*s, interconnected underground water channels will pump in dirty water at all times. We need a citywide underground water decontamination plan. And it is high time that this be pushed to the utmost priority.

Another important aspect to keep in mind is that we no longer have adequate catchment areas around each *baoli*. With carpeted streets and dense concrete jungles, the probability of the underground water table getting recharged naturally is next to zero. Although this problem can be tackled by redirecting the rainwater from rooftops and streets to the underground water table, it also requires a major infrastructural change. More than the financial and logistical challenge, this requires political will.

THE *BAOLIS* OF DELHI

The following list of *baoli*s has been prepared after consulting the historic records of ASI and books like *Monuments of Delhi: Lasting Splendour of the Great Mughals and Others* (1916) by Maulvi Zafar Hasan, *Asar-us-Sanadid* (1847) by Sir Syed Ahmad Khan, and *Waqiaat-e-Darul Hukumat Delhi* (1919) by Bashir-ud-Din Ahmad. Many *baoli*s had no formal name given to them. With time, they were referred using the name of nearby village/locality. However, since the names and boundaries have changed to a great extent, and many new structures have come up around these *baoli*s, most names mentioned in the given table are modern for the ease of the reader, so that one can easily identify the structures. However, official names, as recorded in current government records, have been used for the *baoli*s that fall under government protection. The list that follows is sorted as per the estimated/known year of construction of the respective *baoli*.

Gandhak ki Baoli

Location	Condition as on November 2018	Access
On the crossing of Dargah Road, turning to Dargah of Khwaja Kaki, Mehrauli	Contains water; used for bathing	Open to public

Palam Baoli

Location	Condition as on November 2018	Access
In Palam village, near Babri Mosque; said to have important inscriptions which were lost by early 1900s	Lost/buried	None

Adhchini Baoli

Location	Condition as on November 2018	Access
Near the enclosure of the dargah of Bibi Zulaikha, mother of Hazrat Nizam-ud-Din	Lost/buried	None

Hazrat Nizamuddin Baoli

Location	Condition as on November 2018	Access
At the Northern Gate of Nizam-ud-Din Dargah Complex	Good; water used for bathing	Open to public

Tughlaqabad Baoli 1

Location	Condition as on November 2018	Access
Along the southern wall, walking westward from the present visitors entry	Dry	Open to public

Tughlaqabad Baoli 2

Location	Condition as on November 2018	Access
In the main citadel, towards south-east	Dilapidated; dry	Open to public

Kotla Feroz Shah Baoli

Location	Condition as on November 2018	Access
North-west of the pyramidal structure inside Feroz Shah Kotla Citadel	Good; water being used	Access granted with permission from ASI

Ridge Baoli

Location	Condition as on November 2018	Access
Between the main building of Hindu Rao Hospital and Pir Ghaib; opposite the residential complex of the hospital	Contains clean water; not being used	Open to public

Red Fort Baoli

Location	Condition as on November 2018	Access
Northern area of Red Fort, outside Mehtab Bagh, on track to Salimgarh	Good; water being used	Access granted with permission from ASI

Ugrasen ki Baoli

Location	Condition as on November 2018	Access
Hailey Road, connecting Kasturba Gandhi Marg and Barakhamba Road	Dry	Open to public

Banjaron ki Baoli

Location	Condition as on November 2018	Access
Hidden under a large floor of the historic Matiya Mahal Mosque; a small window on the floor and another on the sidewall under the mosque gives a glimpse of the *baoli* well and pipes pumping the water out	Contains water; pumped through pipes and supplied to Matia Mahal	Closed completely; well visible from a small window

Moradabad Pahari Baoli

Location	Condition as on November 2018	Access
Inside Qasai Wala Gumbad Complex, Moradabad Pahari, Vasant Vihar	Dry or is filled by rainwater	Closed (private property)

Qadam Sharif Baoli

Location	Condition as on November 2018	Access
Inside Qadam Sharif enclosure, Paharganj	Lost/buried	None

Lado Sarai Baoli

Location	Condition as on November 2018	Access
Behind Ahinsa Sthal	Lost/buried	None

Talimabad Baoli

Location	Condition as on November 2018	Access
Inside Hamdard Education Society Complex, Talimabad	Dry	Private property

Baoli near Kabuliwala

Location	Condition as on November 2018	Access
In Mehrauli village, next to the enclosure known as Kabuliwala	Lost/buried	None

Teghanpur Baoli

Location	Condition as on November 2018	Access
Possibly somewhere near Sector 10 metro station, Dwarka	Lost/buried	None

Kharera Baoli

Location	Condition as on November 2018	Access
Near Chor Minar, Hauz Khas Enclave (area originally known as Kharera)	Lost/buried	None

Sultanpur Baoli

Location	Condition as on November 2018	Access
Inside a farmhouse in Sultanpur on Mehrauli–Gurgaon Road	Unsure	None

Basti Baoli

Location	Condition as on November 2018	Access
Defence Colony; inside Defence Colony Mosque (originally tomb and mosque of Khwaja Sara Basti Khan, Raipur Khurd)	Lost/buried	None

Kotla Mubarakpur Baoli

Location	Condition as on November 2018	Access
To north-west of Kotla Mubarakpur; only the edge of the well is visible now	Lost/buried	None

Rajon ki Baoli

Location	Condition as on November 2018	Access
Towards the western end of Mehrauli Archaeological Park	Contains dirty water; not used	Open to public

Munirka Baoli

Location	Condition as on November 2018	Access
Also known as Baoli of Wazirpur Gumbad Complex—Sector 5, R.K. Puram	Dry	Open to public

Loharheri Baoli

Location	Condition as on November 2018	Access
Dwarka Sector 12; between Dwarka International School and Gangotri Apartment, on Azad Hind Fauj Marg	Dry	Open to public

Purana Qila Baoli

Location	Condition as on November 2018	Access
To south-west of Qila-i-Kuhna Mosque inside Purana Qila (Old Fort)	Little water; being used	Access granted with permission from ASI

Khari Baoli

Location	Condition as on November 2018	Access
Under the present Khari Baoli Market, behind Fatehpuri Masjid, Old Delhi	Lost/buried	None

Arab Sarai ki Baoli

Location	Condition as on November 2018	Access
In a less-visited compound (known as Meherban Agha's Market), south of Arab Sarai, Humayun Tomb Complex	Contains water; not used	Access granted with permission from ASI

Aurangzeb ki Baoli

Location	Condition as on November 2018	Access
Near Zafar Mahal, towards the west	Lost/buried	None

Khairpur Baoli

Location	Condition as on November 2018	Access
Inside Lodhi Gardens, right outside the mosque and the rose garden (Lodhi Gardens was built by relocating a village known as Khairpur)	Lost/buried	None

Zeenat Begum Baoli

Location	Condition as on November 2018	Access
Next to Zeenat Begum's mosque, Aliganj (now Jor Bagh)	Lost/buried	None

Hakim ji's Baoli

Location	Condition as on November 2018	Access
Next to the mosque in Hakim ji's garden in Raisina village (exact location of garden unknown)	Lost/buried	None

Dawood ki Baoli or Qutb Sahib ki Baoli

Location	Condition as on November 2018	Access
Inside the dargah, under the southern courtyard outside Majlis Khana	Contains dirty water; not used	Access granted with permission from Dargah Committee

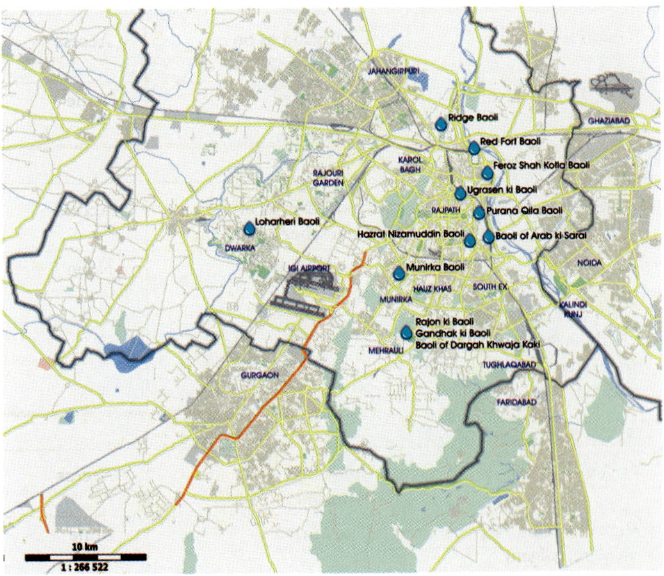

Map of the *baolis* of Delhi

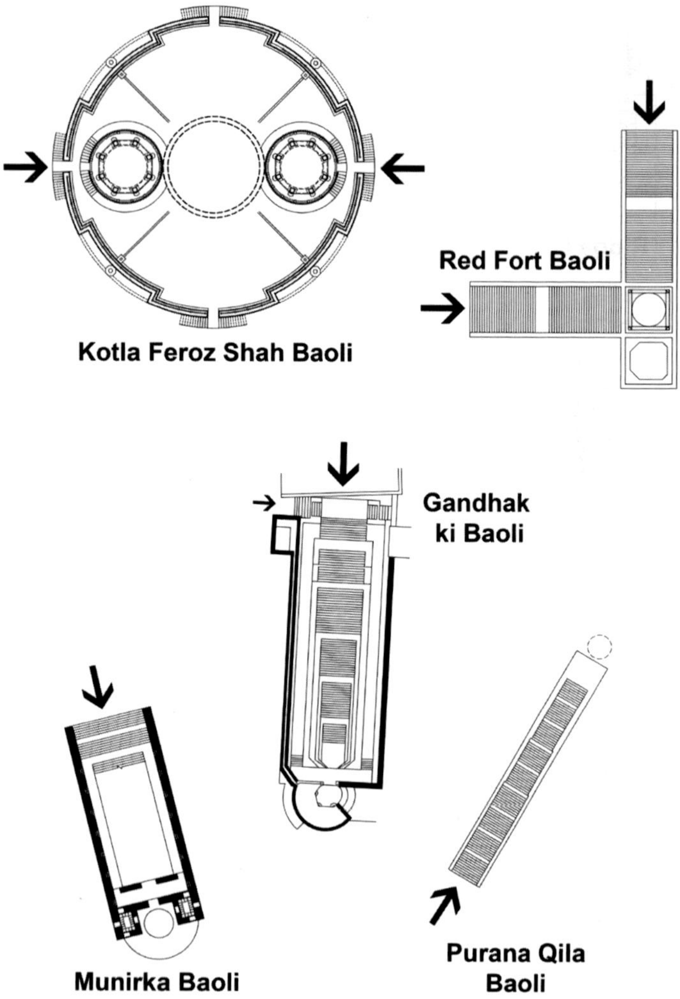

The illustration shows the top ten *baolis* relative to each other

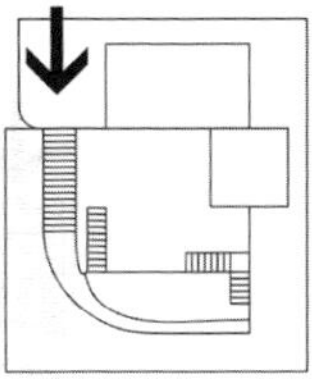

Ridge Baoli

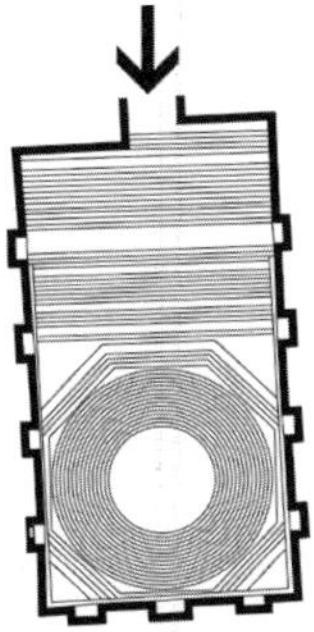

Hazrat Nizam-ud-Din Baoli

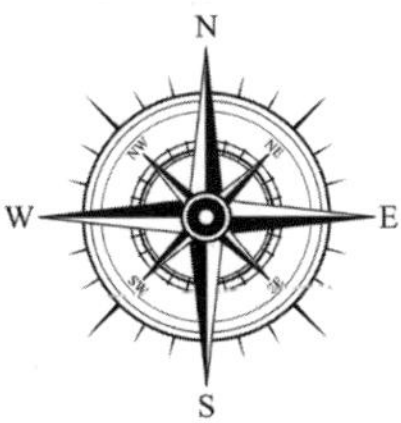

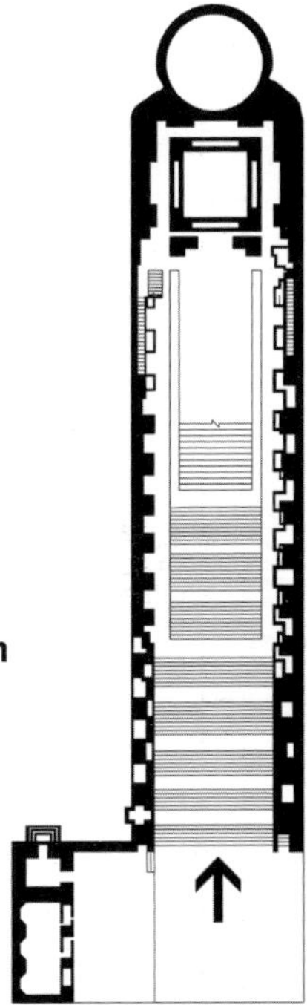

Ugrasen ki Baoli

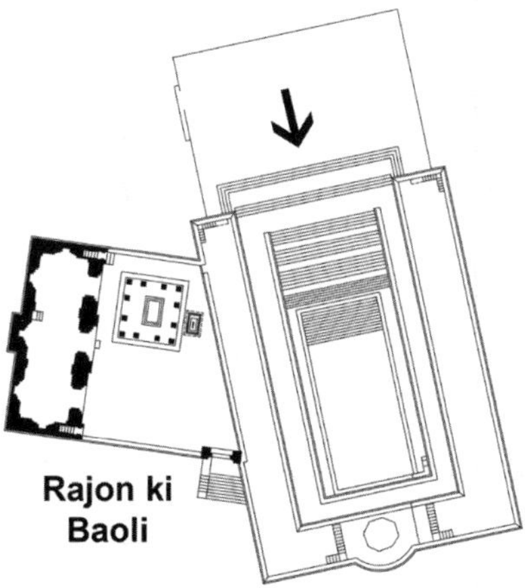

Rajon ki Baoli

Loharheri Baoli

Disclaimer: All illustrations not to scale

KOTLA FEROZ SHAH BAOLI

फ़िरोज़ शाह कोटला की बावली فروز شاہ کوٹلا کی باولی ਫ਼ਿਰੋਜ਼ ਸ਼ਾਹ ਕੋਟਲਾ ਦੀ ਬਾਉਲੀ

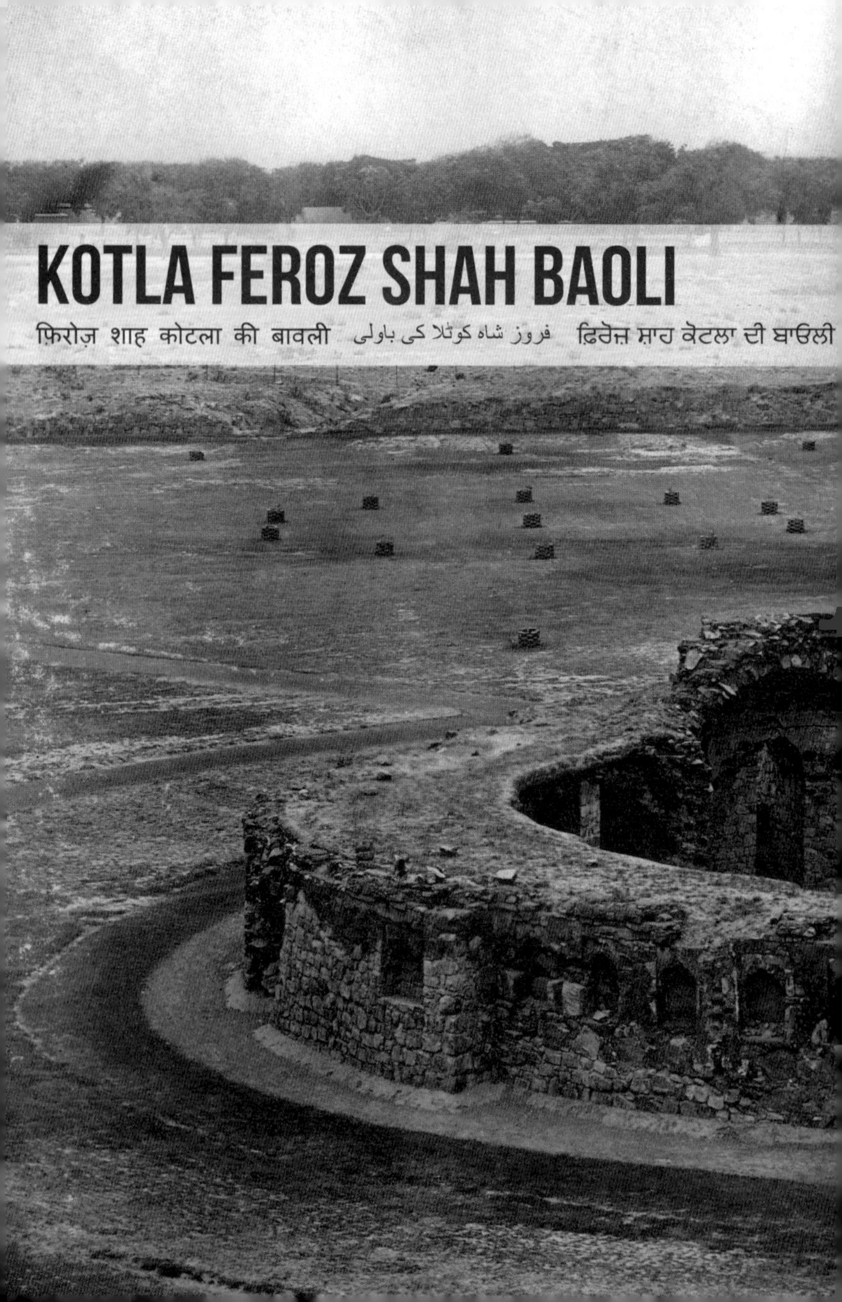

A panoramic view of the Kotla Feroz Shah Baoli in 2018

Previous page: An extensive view of the Kotla Feroz Shah Baoli in 1923. The picture has been taken from the edge of the pyramidal structure in the fort. *Source: ASI Photo Archives*

Feroz Shah Tughlaq (r. 1351–1388) took special interest in strengthening the infrastructure of his empire. Not only did he build new structures, but also invested time and money in repairing buildings built by his predecessors. One of the best examples would be the Qutub Minar, which was extended by Tughlaq to its present state consisting of five storeys. Feroz Shah is more famous for commissioning buildings of architectural shapes that were seen as unconventional during his era. He is also considered the father of the irrigation system in India for channelizing rivers to provide water through canals to a large part of the country.

Feroz Shah Tughlaq came to power after the death of his cousin, Sultan Muhammad Bin Tughlaq. Muhammad Bin Tughlaq was known to be a lunatic king. His decision left the treasury dry and the economy collapsing. Feroz Shah avoided the throne for a long time, but due to pressure from the nobles, he eventually agreed to be the third sultan of the Tughlaq dynasty.

Instead of wars, he decided to spend more time and money on city planning, construction of public buildings, roads, water channels, and utilities. One of his commissioned structures is the *baoli* inside the citadel of Ferozabad. The citadel is known as Kotla-i-Feroz Shahi (the fortress of Feroz Shah), but more commonly referred to as Feroz Shah Kotla. Today, this fort is the favourite destination for those who believe in djinns and want to have their wishes granted or their problems solved. You can see devotees sitting

View of the *baoli* with the Ashokan Pillar above the pyramidal structure visible in the background

in almost every corner, lighting earthen lamps or incense sticks and praying to djinns. But what may amuse some first-time visitors is that many devotees also write their prayers on a piece of paper and stick them on the walls. Of late, people have also started lighting a lamp in a small window on the outer wall of the *baoli*.

This *baoli* is situated right before the pyramidal structure, containing the Ashokan Pillar, which

A stunning view of the *baoli* as seen from the remains of the Eastern Tower

The corridor and the ramp leading to the Western Tower and the tank of the *baoli*

Steps leading down to the lower level of the *baoli*

Tughlaq brought from Topra near Jagadhri, Haryana. It is the only circular *baoli*/tank in Delhi. Other nearby circular ones are Surajkund in Faridabad and Pir Ghaus Ali Shah's *baoli* in Farrukhnagar, Gurgaon—both in Haryana. The *baoli* of Feroz Shah Kotla measures 33 metres in diameter on the outside, and the water tank is around 9 metres. Area wise, this makes it the largest *baoli* in Delhi.

What adds to the uniqueness of this *baoli* is the fact that it is not like most other *baoli*s of Delhi, where the well is separated from the tank by a wall. In this case,

A flight of stairs running up the *baoli*

Remains of the Western Tower

it is just the well dug up to form a tank. Other such examples in Delhi are the Nizam-ud-Din Baoli and the *baoli*s of Tughlaqabad Fort. We are not comparing Feroz Shah Kotla Baoli with a kund, as this one has subterranean apartments and was once covered with a roof. These two elements are, however, missing in Nizam-ud-Din and Tughlaqabad *baoli*s. It also has an underground drainpipe leading to the Yamuna. There is a possibility that the roof had a small opening in the centre. We cannot be sure of this, as the entire roof has collapsed now with no written description of the actual architecture. Originally, it had entry from the east and the west, but only the west side is open now for public. As you enter, the flight of steps takes you to the lower level where you can access apartments and the water tank. Towards the east and the west, above the entrances, it once had two domed *chhatris* with stairs on either side.

Location	Inside Feroz Shah Kotla (citadel)
Period	AD 1354 (Feroz Shah Tughlaq)
Public Access	With permission from ASI
Managing Authority	Archaeological Survey of India
Water Level	High
Latitude–Longitude	28.636012, 77.244668
Nearest Metro Station	Delhi Gate Metro Station
Distance to Nearest Metro Station	700 metres (approx.)

A stone pillar supporting the roof of the Western Tower

Exit to the tank. Sometimes, the chamber gets submerged when the water level surges.

A magnificent view of the circular *baoli* with dilapidated edges and collapsed high walls

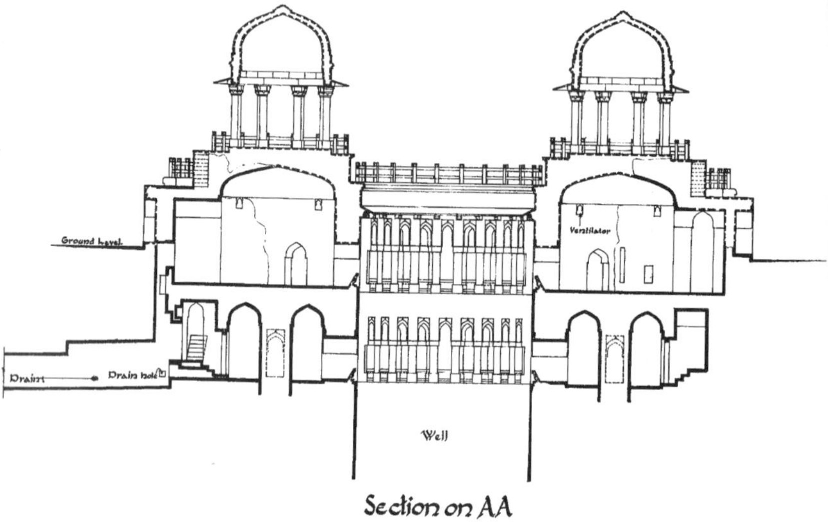

Conjectural drawing prepared by the Archaeological Survey of India before 1919, based on architectural remains and historic records.
Source: ASI Photo Archives

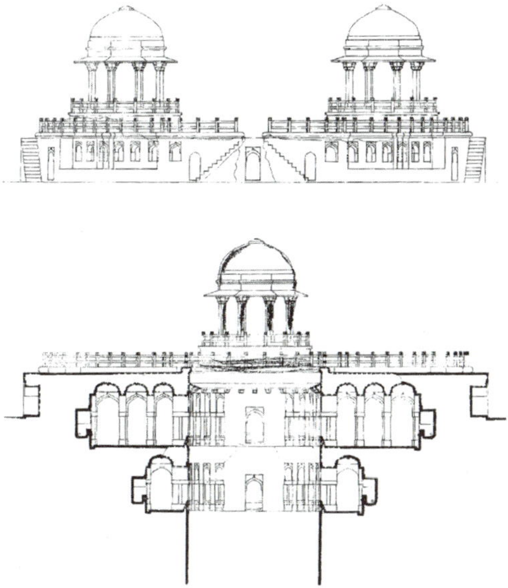

A sketch of the restored front elevation and cross section of the tower, prepared by the Archaeological Survey of India sometime before 1919.
Source: ASI Photo Archives

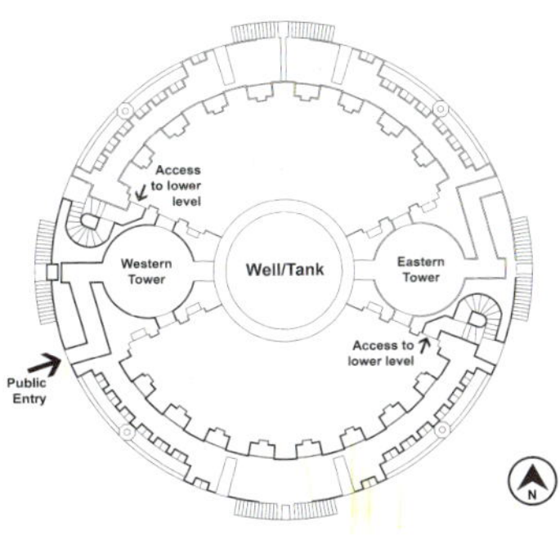

Sectional top view based on the drawings of the Archaeological Survey of India

RED FORT BAOLI

लाल किले की बावली   لال قلہ کی باولی   ਲਾਲ ਕਿਲੇ ਦੀ ਬਾਓਲੀ

On 12 May 1639, the foundation of Qila-i-Mu'alla (now known as Red Fort) was laid. The area marked for the imperial palace of the mighty Mughals was on the land that was once a part of Feroz Shah Tughlaq's city Ferozabad. The city was no longer in its original shape. But one important structure, almost 300 years older than the foundation day, was kept intact in the plan of this palace. This structure was the *baoli* that we now know as the Red Fort Baoli, arguably the most well-kept of all *baoli*s in Delhi. While few historians question the association of Tughlaq with this *baoli*, there are several others who prove the claim. Dr Narayani Gupta and Ratish Nanda, in their listing of Delhi's monuments in the book *Delhi, The Built Heritage* (1999), have categorized it as a Tughlaq-period *baoli*. Maulvi Zafar Hasan, in his record (*Monuments of Delhi: Lasting Splendour of the Great Mughals and the Others*), mentions it as 'late Afghan', but also places a question mark next to it, indicating his doubt over the assumption. Surprisingly, this *baoli* finds very little mention in other historic documents of British or Mughal era, despite being a prominent structure at a prominent location. Bashir-ud-Din Ahmad, in his work *Waqiaat-e-Darul Hukumat Delhi*, notes that the *baoli* in Red Fort has stairs leading to the tank from the two sides, but is covered, and the water is used to irrigate the gardens of the Red Fort. However, he makes no mention of the origin or construction of this *baoli*. Looking at the fine work of this *baoli*, one can debate that it was not constructed during the Tughlaq period. It appears to be built during Lodhi or Mughal era. However, such a statement is hypothetic in the absence of any definitive records present. There is also a possibility of a structure which might have been built over or repaired with better masonry later.

As you enter from the Lahori Gate of the Red Fort and cross Chhatta Chowk, you reach an open compound, which further leads to Naubat Khana. From this compound, if you turn left (instead of proceeding

A flight of steps leading down to the water tank. The structure over the well is visible in the upper right corner.

Previous page: A view of the stone stairway seen through the archway of the Eastern Chamber of the Red Fort Baoli

towards Naubat Khana), the road takes you to the *baoli*, crossing a few British barracks. This road was once arcaded and had another gate at the end, outside which the *baoli* is situated. The arcades, gate, and all other buildings were destroyed by the British after the events of 1857. Later, barracks were constructed, and a parade ground was built in the cleared area.

Left: Perpendicular staircases, descending from two sides, intersect at the tank that holds the water. The staircases are lined with chambers on both sides.

Right: The octagonal shaft of the well. A platform was built by the British to prevent people from falling in. Water can be seen through the two openings made for cleaning the water.

This *baoli* qualifies as a unique architectural experiment, as it has two flights of stairs—from the west and from the north—connecting the water basin mirrored at ninety degrees. It is a rare L-shape, which strengthens our belief about this structure being a Tughlaq-era construction, as, during Feroz Shah's reign, several architectural experiments were carried out.

Side chambers, converted to prison cells, where the officers of the Indian National Army were confined by the British

To its south, a 46’10” deep octagonal shaft of 21’4” diameter serves as the well. A tank of the *baoli* measures 20’ by 20’ and is at a depth of 27’5”. A small, arched window between the well and the tank allows water to transfer.

It is rather amusing to learn that people in those days built a *baoli* for the public, hardly hundred

Corridor connecting the chambers that served as a prison

metres away from the Yamuna. There is a possibility that the medieval people found some minerals in Yamuna that were/are unsafe for daily consumption, or simply the brackish nature of Yamuna prevented them from using the water regularly. May be, that was why they relied more on the water of the wells and *baolis*, where it got filtered by sand.

When the British army converted this fort into its permanent cantonment, they covered this *baoli* with iron girders, leaving only the first level accessible. Pipes were pushed into the well and water was pumped out using motors. Later, on 6 July 1945, Gurbaksh Singh Dhillon, Shah Nawaz Khan, and Prem Kumar Sahgal, the three brave commanders of Netaji Subhas Chandra Bose's Indian National Army, were brought to the Red Fort. This *baoli* served as a jail for them. Arches were sealed with brick walls. Small guarded doors and windows were built, confining these special prisoners. A makeshift toilet was also made inside these dark cells. Later, the trio was tried in the Salimgarh Fort, situated behind Red Fort. These covered arches and windows with bars still exist there.

After 1947, the Indian Army continued to occupy the Red Fort and the *baoli* was forgotten. Vegetation

An arched entrance opening into the water tank. The octagonal shaft of the well is visible behind the arches.

A small temple operating in the outer southern arch of the *baoli* well

grew over it, and it was nothing more than a garbage dumping ground. In 2002, the army handed over this fort to the ASI, who was preparing it to be the next World Heritage Site. The ASI started desilting and removing the encroachments, which took several months. The original plan of the ASI was to convert this *baoli* into a memorial for the army, but given the sensitive structure and threat of snakes all around, the idea was never executed. Instead, a nice museum was put up in Salimgarh, a stone's throw away from this *baoli*. The iron girders that were removed are kept in one corner of the *baoli*. Few more buildings built by the army right on the edge of the *baoli* were removed during the restoration in 2018–19.

In 2012, the water pockets around the well were much higher than the level of water in it. One could hence hear spouts of water falling in from a height into the *baoli*. The scenario changed in 2016 when, during the construction of Delhi Metro's Heritage Line, the workers accidentally punctured the underground water

An unknown grave, situated under the outer eastern arch of the *baoli* well

channel. This resulted in draining of the underground waterway, and it dried up the *baoli*. The mistake was detected and rectified, and water returned to the *baoli* in less than a year.

Another interesting element in this *baoli* is that the octagonal shaft of the well has a small walled structure on top of it. This structure used to hold the Persian Wheel with which people used to pull water out of this *baoli*. Towards the southern and eastern sides, the wall has tiny arcaded rooms. On the southern side, we have a small temple functioning, while on the eastern side, there is a grave. There is absolutely no documentation of their origin or even existence. It appears to be from the times of the Indian Army and is currently maintained by the local staff.

Entrance through the archway framing the beautiful *baoli*, as seen from the Eastern Chamber

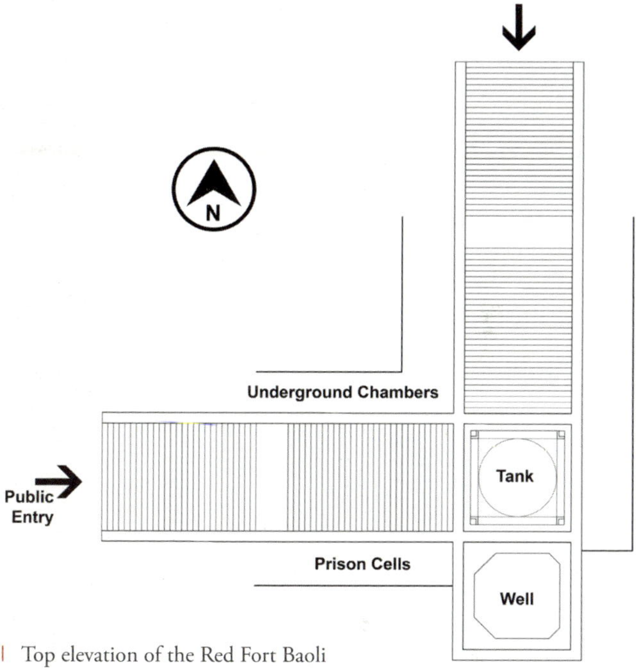

Top elevation of the Red Fort Baoli

Location	Salimgarh Road, Inside Red Fort
Period	Tughlaq–Sur–Mughal
Public Access	With permission from ASI
Managing Authority	Archaeological Survey of India
Water Level	Dried up in 2016; revived the same year
Latitude–Longitude	28.658984, 77.240581
Nearest Metro Station	Lal Qila Metro Station
Distance to Nearest Metro Station	350 metres (approx.)

RIDGE BAOLI

रिज बावली　　ہندو راوکی باولی　　ਰਿਜ ਬਾਓਲੀ

A sweeping view of the Ridge Baoli with possible arched chambers and recently restored contours and steps

Previous page: The *baoli* in Hindu Rao Hospital, as captured in January 2011, with its archaic architecture and chambers supposed to be once around it

Another interesting structure commissioned by Sultan Feroz Shah Tughlaq is the *baoli* which now falls inside the premises of Hindu Rao Hospital in North Delhi. It is situated right next to Pir Ghaib, an observatory built by Tughlaq. We also get a reference to an important palace or a hunting lodge by the name Kushk-i-Shikaar or the Jehan Numa Palace around this area, which is lost with time. Pir Ghaib is probably what is left of that palace. The *baoli* was intended to supply water to this imperial abode.

Records suggest that this *baoli* was surrounded by a series of chambers, like the other *baoli*s of Tughlaq's period. However, all these rooms have now disappeared. On the top, there are traces of tiny reservoirs with aqueducts that must have been used to supply water to Feroz Shah's nearby palace. By the end of the nineteenth century, the British discovered a tunnel running through this *baoli*. Abu'l Fazl, the author of *Ain-i-Akbari*, suggests that Feroz Shah Tughlaq built a tunnel from his city Ferozabad to the Jehan Numa Palace. However, when archaeologists examined the tunnel, they found it to be too narrow and low to fit the description given by Abu'l Fazl. He mentions that Feroz Shah could pass this tunnel, mounted on his horse, with the proper procession. The tunnel found by the British was cleared to the depth of around 633 feet to the north, terminating at a small doorway of local hardstone measuring 3 feet by 1 feet 9 inches. Records suggest that the tunnel appeared to be continuing further in that direction, but had dilapidated walls which were low and untimely. These walls disappear at 96 feet into the rock bed of the ridge. However, at a depth of 25 feet

The monumental structure of rubble masonry, with a major arch visible on the left and the water pool at the bottom

inside the terminating doorway, as mentioned earlier, there is another doorway of hardstone measuring 4 feet 8 inches by 2 feet 5 inches. The portion between the two gateways is covered with a flat roof made of stone slabs. The remainder of the tunnel has a vaulted roof. British accounts also suggest that the tunnel originally contained eight light or ventilation shafts, out of which they opened only six. At the entrance, the tunnel is just 2 feet wide and 7 feet 2 inches high, but the height is not uniform throughout the

The Ridge Baoli with its arches and pillars that held the structure intact. The location of the tunnel amongst these arches is unknown.

Part of the building that earlier served as Fraser's House and then the *bara* of Raja Hindu Rao

passage. It becomes so low at intervals that a person cannot stand straight inside it. It goes as low as 4 feet 10 inches at one point.

In the premises, there used to be the house of William Fraser which was later purchased by the brother-in-law of Maharaja Daulat Rao Scindia of Gwalior, Raja Hindu Rao. It suffered a lot during the 1857 conflicts.

The entrance to Pir Ghaib, the observatory that is believed to be a part of Kushk-i-Jahanuma

This building was later restored and when the hospital was established, it served as the plastic ward (sic) and the ENT ward. As of today, it is the office of the North DMC Medical College, operating inside Hindu Rao Hospital.

Another very important building right next to this *baoli* is an observatory that we know as Pir Ghaib, literally, the saint who disappeared. This building is contemporary of the *baoli* and appears to have been much larger than what stands now. There is a possibility that Pir Ghaib is either part of Jehan Numa Palace or one of the buildings in its complex. The construction of such a big *baoli* next to a hunting lodge suggests that this area was not merely for hunting. What would surprise anyone inside this building is a cenotaph on the upper level. Tradition avers that this room was the worshipping place of a saint, who suddenly vanished one day. Later, a cenotaph was constructed there in his memory, but due to lack of space in the room, the cenotaph was constructed from west to east, contrary to Islamic practice.

Another important structure in the vicinity is the Ashokan Pillar, which stands few metres away from these buildings. Feroz Shah Tughlaq brought in two pillars, one from Meerut and another from Jagadhri (Haryana), which he planted in two of his palaces. One being the Kotla-i-Feroz Shahi, and other being Kushk-i-Jahanuma.

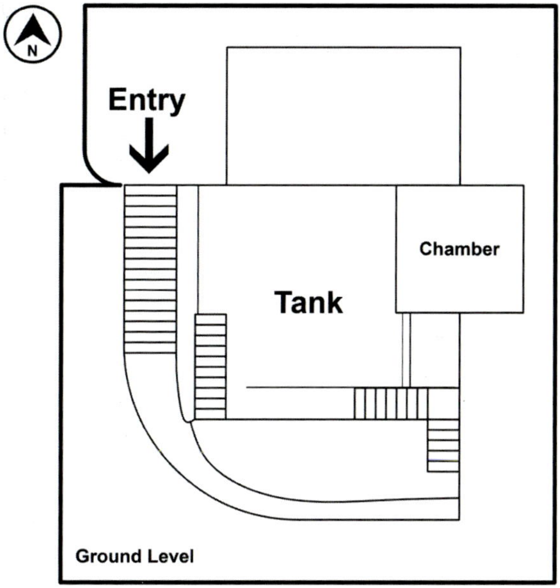

Plan of Ridge Baoli

Location	Inside Hindu Rao Hospital
Period	Feroz Shah Tughlaq
Public Access	Allowed
Managing Authority	Archaeological Survey of India
Water Level	Filled with rainwater
Latitude–Longitude	28.676248, 77.212746
Nearest Metro Station	Pulbangash Metro Station
Distance to Nearest Metro Station	1.25 kms (approx.)

HAZRAT NIZAM-UD-DIN BAOLI

हज़रत निजामुद्दीन की बावली حضرت نظاملدین کی باولی ਹਜ਼ਰਤ ਨਿਜ਼ਾਮੁਦੀਨ ਦੀ ਬਾਓਲੀ

As the story goes, the construction of a *baoli* in Ghyaspura (now Hazrat Nizam-ud-Din Basti or Nizam-ud-Din West) was underway, when Sultan Ghiyas-ud-Din Tughlaq's ambitious project Tughlaqabad began. Tughlaq forced all the available labour to work only for Tughlaqabad, and the work at the *baoli* was stalled. Khwaja Nizam-ud-Din Auliya, fourth in the Chishti order of Sufism in India, requested masons to work at the *baoli* during late hours after their shift in Tughlaqabad. He was a beloved of everyone, so the masons agreed to do the job. One day, a supervisor found one of the masons sleeping during his day shift. Upon inquiry, the covert double shift plan was revealed. Tughlaq got so angry that he prohibited the sale of burning oil in the region. Without oil, earthen lamps could not be lit, and without light, no one could work at night. It is said that Hazrat Nizam-ud-Din Auliya cursed the fort of Tughlaqabad and suggested his disciple Hazrat Nasiruddin to attempt lighting the lamps with the *baoli*'s water. People say that Hazrat Nasiruddin, who later became Nizam-ud-Din's successor, illuminated the village by lighting lamps filled with mere water.

He was thus given the title of Roshan Chiragh-e-Dehli (the light of Delhi). The water of this *baoli* is considered miraculous thenceforth. One variation of this story is found in the record of Zafar Hasan, where he mentions that when Ghiyas-ud-Din prohibited the sale of oil in the region, Nizam-ud-Din complained to Sayyid Muhammad Behar, who was building a mud wall. The latter, angered at the emperor's persecution

View of the *baoli* from the south-east corner, with the iconic five-arched pavilion at the back and Chini ka Rauza above the steps

Previous page: Daniel's painting of Nizam-ud-Din Baoli in British Library. *Source: Copy from ASI Photo Archives*

of the saint, demolished his mud wall and exclaimed, 'I have destroyed his empire!' Other writers attribute this incident to Hazrat Nizam-ud-Din and say that the saint cursed the city of Tughlaqabad with the words, '*Ya rahe ujjad, ya base gujjar*', implying that the city will either remain in ruins or be populated by herders.

This is a story that the people of Delhi will narrate to you with pride. However, such stories are often regarded as hearsay and discarded by credible historians. But they remain an important part of the oral traditions of a community and say a lot about the era. Such stories sometimes also fall prey to Chinese whispers. Going by the recorded information,

Left to right: A 1902 view of the north wall of the *baoli*, showing the Lal Chaubara, tombs of Fatima Bibi and Zuhra Aga, and Chini ka Rauza. *Source: ASI Photo Archives*

A 1916 view of the *baoli*. The five arches towards the west do not have jalis, but three of them are closed with bricks. *Source: ASI Photo Archives*

A 1919 view of the *baoli*'s entrance. Notice the boys standing atop Chini ka Rauza. As recorded by many, local boys used to jump into the *baoli* from adjoining buildings for the amusement of visitors. *Source: ASI Photo Archives*

many historians and archaeologists noted that this *baoli* was built in AD 1321–22, during the lifetime of Khwaja Nizam-ud-Din Auliya. Khwaja Nizam-ud-Din started removing the mud with his own hands, thus marking the beginning. In 1379, one Muhammad

Maruf, son of the minister Wahiduddin Qureshi, built mud houses in the nearby streets of this *baoli* and inscribed the name of Feroz Shah Tughlaq on a stone slab. Sir Syed Ahmad mentions seeing this slab (mid-nineteenth century). He also says that there are several graves and dwellings around the *baoli*. The wall around the *baoli* (and the shrine) was built by Nawab Ahmad Baksh Khan of Ferozepur. To the south of the *baoli*, there is an arcaded chamber adorned with pierced, red-sandstone jalis. Originally, these arches were not sealed with jalis and were just covered with small stone parapets to prevent one from falling into the *baoli*. While experts like Maulvi Zafar Hasan find this structure of no interest, I think that this chamber is one of the most important aesthetic elements of the *baoli*. The *baoli* today is recognized due to this chamber and its five windows. Other important structures comprising the *baoli* wall are the tombs of Fatima Bibi and Zuhra Aga in the north-west corner, Chini ka Burj to the west, Bai Kodaldai's Tomb to the west, and a building called Lal Chaubara to the north-west. Some of these buildings are dilapidated beyond recognition, and a few even lost. On the eastern side is the passage to enter the dargah. The *baoli* is accessed through a small gate from the north.

Further reference to the slab mentioned by Sir Syed Ahmad Khan can be found in the book by Maulvi Zafar Hasan mentioned before. While Zafar Hasan clearly states that there are no inscriptions on the *baoli*, he referes to a slab in the southern arcaded building which matches the description by Sir Syed Ahmad. The translation, as given by Zafar Hasan, follows:

In the name of God who is merciful and clement.
In the reign of the great king, the fortunate monarch and the descendant of Adam,
The support of the religion of Ahmad (the Prophet), Firoz Shah who is a king, Lord of the happy constellation and the greatest of sovereigns,
The slave Maruf was assisted by God, and he made firm the foundation of this building,
In the neighbourhood of the tomb of Shaikhul Mashayakh Nizamul Haq-Wa-deen, the pole star of the world,
Wahiduddin Quraishi, my father, who was a companion of the devotees (of Shaikh Nizam-ud-Din),
And who was a confidant in the secrets of the friend of God (Nizam-ud-Din) of good faith and sincerity,
When he brought me before the chief of the world (Nizam-ud-Din), he (the latter) took me in his arms and named me.
And the Shaikh with the breath of Jesus named me Maruf in his own utterance, in this world.

I hope through that auspicious utterance to attain to fame in the next world also.
Read the date of the completion of this building as a welcome when you visit this place.
It was seven hundred and eighty-one from Hijrat when this building was erected. God knows best.

This slab no longer exists. But the empty space (usually meant for such slabs) outside the south gate (towards the dargah) of the *baoli* chamber confirms the story.

As you enter the dargah complex from the northern gate, the first structure you encounter is this *baoli*. It measures 123 feet by 53 feet internally. This *baoli* has one similarity with the Kotla Feroz Shah Baoli. There is no separate well (like other *baolis*), but the tank is the well. One major difference from Kotla Feroz Shah is that Nizam-ud-Din Baoli is not covered.

Location	North gate of Dargah Nizam-ud-Din
Period	Ghiyas-ud-Din Tughlaq Shah I
Public Access	Allowed
Managing Authority	Dargah Committee
Water Level	Filled with unclean water
Latitude-Longitude	28.591860, 77.241919
Nearest Metro Station	JLN Stadium Metro Station
Distance to Nearest Metro Station	1.2 kms (approx.)

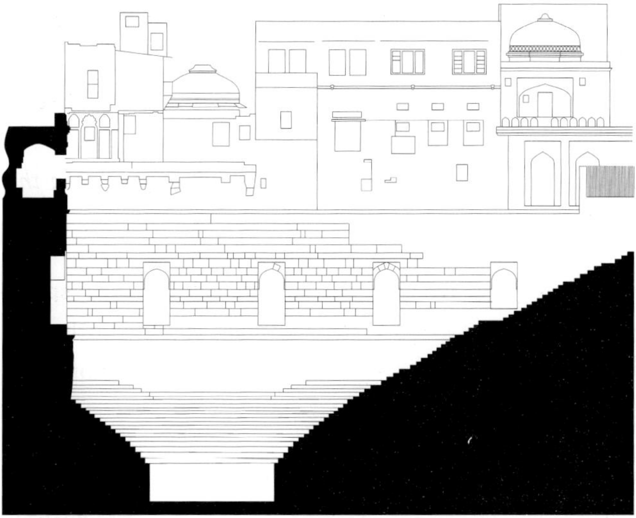

Cross section of the Nizam-ud-Din Baoli

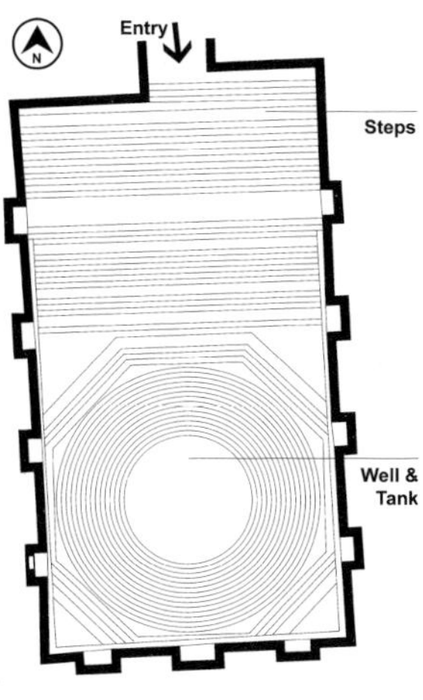

General plan of the Nizam-ud-Din Baoli

UGRASEN KI BAOLI

उग्रसेन की बावली اگرسین کی باولی ਉਗ੍ਰਸੇਨ ਦੀ ਬਾਓਲੀ

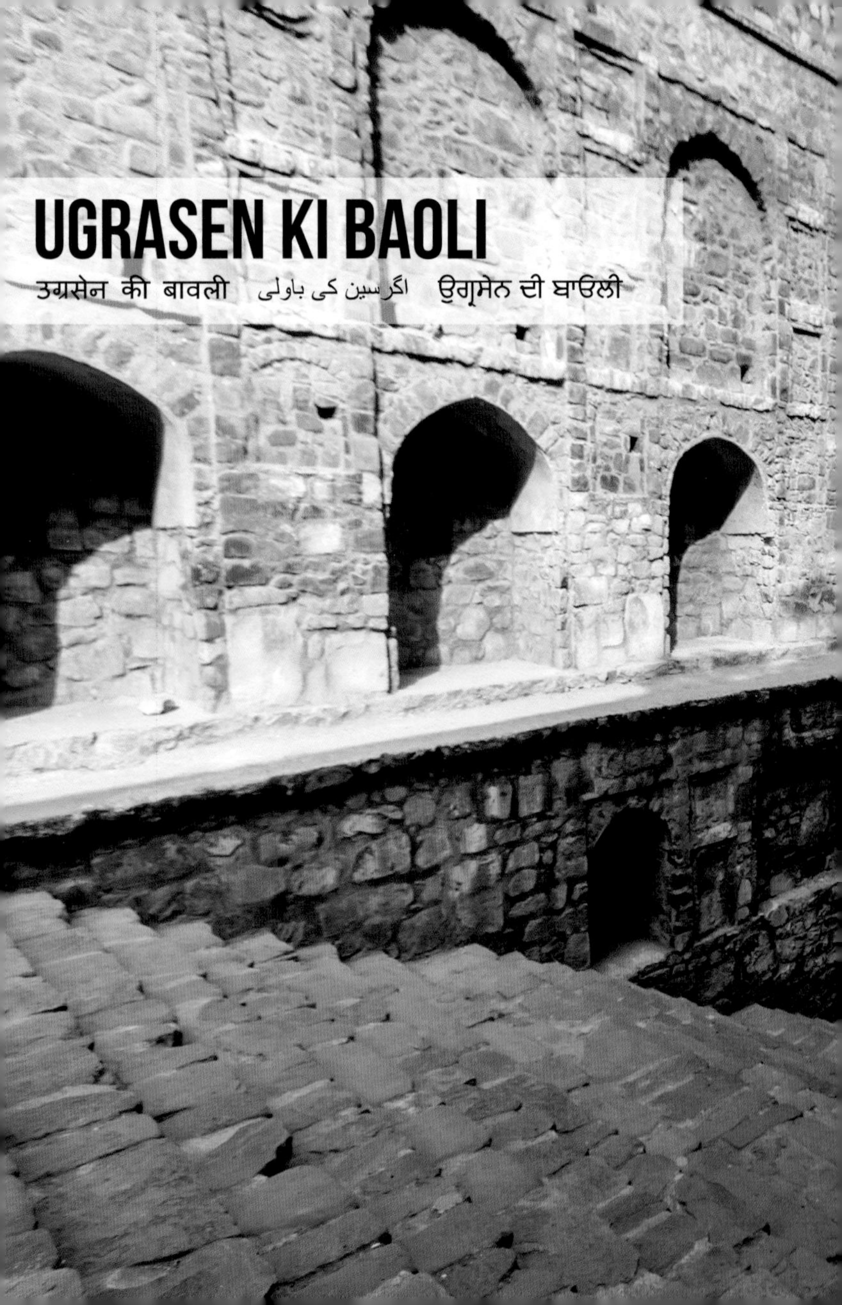

The most famous *baoli* in Delhi, especially after actor Aamir Khan posed there in his movie *PK*, is the *baoli* on Hailey Lane, popularly known as Ugrasen ki Baoli. Though, in terms of popularity, it deserves to be ranked as number one in the list, it failed on the parameters of water level and usage, and hence slipped to rank five. It is rather interesting to see how the title starts with 'U' and not with 'A'. This largely reflects the dialect of medieval Delhi and how it changed over time. We must not forget that during Mughal times, the court language was Persian before one of the emperors decided to switch to Urdu. Later, when the British took over, they translated essential records from Urdu to English. Most of our spellings

Left: The name stone outside the *baoli*, installed by the authorities

Previous page: A panoramic shot of Ugrasen ki Baoli, lined with arches along the western wall. One can see the three storeys visible.

in English reflect the phonetic sounds, as British and their Indian employees interpreted back then.

The Kasturba Gandhi Marg (formerly Curzon Road) and Barakhamba Road are connected via Hailey Road, named after Lord William Malcolm Hailey, governor of Punjab and later of United Provinces (parts of Uttar Pradesh and Uttarakhand). As you turn from K.G. Marg on to Hailey Road, the first cut to your left (known as Hailey Lane), after approximately a hundred metres, takes you to this medieval *baoli*. Archaeologists like Y.D. Sharma are of the opinion that the architectural elements in this *baoli* relate it to Tughlaq era, while some suggest that certain portions appear to be of Lodhi's period. However, folklores attribute this *baoli* to Maharaja Agrasen, who is believed by the Aggarwal community to be their founder. Agrasen's name is referenced in *Mahabharata*, where it is said that he built a garden known as Agravan (now Agra). Samuel Beale (1803-1874), who translated many Chinese travel accounts into English, also suggests that this *baoli* is named after Maharaja Agrasen who ruled Agra several centuries before Sikandar Lodhi. His name is also found in the Sikh holy book *Guru Granth Sahib*, where it appears in the following verse: '*Duapar Krishan muraar, kans kirtarath kiyo, Ugrasen ko raj, abhai bhagateh jan diyo.*'

Maharaja Agrasen is said to have been the ruler of Agroha. It is difficult to estimate the period of his rule, as no concrete record has been found for it. This led several historians to believe that Maharaja Agrasen is nothing but a mythical personality. Those who believe in his existence made several attempts to authenticate him through references found in different scriptures. For example, Bhartendu Harishchandra (1850–1885), in his essay compilation 'Agarwalon ki Utpatti' (1871), claims that Maharaja Agrasen was a contemporary of Krishna. His findings are derived from 'Sri Mahalaxmi Vrat ki Katha' in *Bhavishya Purana* and a few other sources.

Bashir-ud-Din Ahmad has his own view in this regard. He says that, as the name suggests, this *baoli* was built by a Hindu. Given the size of this *baoli*, the builder was no ordinary person. He also adds that since there is a mosque attached to this *baoli*, many people think that either the builder was a Muslim, or some Muslim ruler/noble added the mosque later. But he clarifies that many Hindu nobles were known to construct buildings for other faiths, and we have examples where Hindus have commissioned *imambaras*, dargahs, tombs, and other structures usually associated with Islam. Therefore, it is a possibility that the *baoli*,

A 1914 archival pic, showing overgrown vegetation and the dilapidated *baoli* filled with water. *Source: ASI Photo Archives*

Picture clicked from the same angle in 1926, showing the same level of water. *Source: ASI Photo Archives*

A picture of the *baoli* from 2010, showing the dry and restored *baoli*, with all the four storeys visible

together with its mosque, was built by a Hindu. But interestingly, Ahmad in his book *Waqiaat-e-Darul Hukumat Delhi* spells his name with different spellings each time. One of them is with a 'U'. In Urdu, writers often drop *zabar* and *pesh*, which gives the sound of 'E' and 'U' respectively, unless very important. In this case, he writes the name with a *pesh* on alif, which means it starts with a 'U' and not 'A'. In other cases, the *pesh* (sound of U) is not enforced and is left to the judgement of the reader. But he is completely silent on the date of this *baoli* and does not give any hint if this Ugrasen is the same Maharaja Agrasen. He also mentions an enclosure to the east of this *baoli* and says that there used to be a palatial building inside this enclosure which is now gone. He further adds that the enclosure is now filled with stones and mud, and labour is using this material to construct the road. This book was written in 1919, when roads were being built in the area.

In old records, this *baoli* is said to be in a village called Narhaula near Madhoganj and Jaisinghpura. These names no longer exist, as the villages were consumed when New Delhi was being built. It is said that this land originally belonged to the kings of Jaipur. In the *Constable's Hand Atlas of India* (1893) by

Remains of the mosque at the southern end of the *baoli*

J.G. Bartholomew, this *baoli* is mentioned as Ujar Sain Baoli. In later records, it was spelled as Ugar Sain's Baoli and later Ugrasen ki Baoli. In early 1900s, the then superintending archaeologist of ASI, Maulvi Zafar Hasan, prepared his list on the monuments of Delhi. He mentioned this *baoli* as Agar Sain Baoli. Interestingly, the ASI adopted the nomenclature from Zafar Hasan's listing, but the spellings for this *baoli*'s name were changed.

If we believe oral claims, there is a possibility that the *baoli* existed before Tughlaq's reign. Feroz Shah Tughlaq commissioned the repairing and rebuilding of several structures. He could have restored this *baoli* and added a mosque to it. But we do not have any written evidence to support this claim. During the Lodhi era, further work was carried upon. The original entrance to this *baoli* no longer exists. Currently, the *baoli* measures 192 feet by 45 feet at the ground level and 129 feet 3 inches by

Staircase from the sidewall leading to the upper level of the *baoli*

The view of the *baoli* through the graceful archway and stone steps, as seen from the base of the tank

24 feet by 6 inches at the water level. Towards the north, the length of 33 feet 6 inches is roofed. It is divided into three levels, each one having access to the other via a flight of stairs through the corridors within the walls of the *baoli*. The circular well towards the north is of 25 feet and 6 inches diameter. Both the tank and the well are completely dry. They develop puddles of water during heavy rains. However, we have a few photographs from early 1900s showing the *baoli* filled more than half with water. The mosque towards the south is on a raised platform and has

A 1923 archival picture showing a tree in front of the mosque, which later grew big enough to cover the entire mosque. It still exists.
Source: ASI Photo Archives

three arches, one of which has collapsed. The spandrels are covered with stucco medallions.

Interestingly, the *baoli* has 108 steps. It does not seem to be a deliberate effort, but just the calculation-fitting situation. However, 108 has a major significance in Indian culture. The distance between the earth and the sun is approximately 108 times the diameter of the sun. The distance between the earth and the moon is roughly 108 times the diameter of the moon. According to Indian astrology, there are twelve houses and nine planets (12 times 9 is 108). Again, we have 108 Upanishads in Hinduism. Ayurveda describes 108 Marma points, which are vital for giving life to any living being. *Natya Shastra* of Rishi Bharata has 108 *karana*s (movement of hands and feet). Our sages calculated that there are 108 lies and 108 desires of mortals.

Few dwellings can be spotted around this *baoli* in a picture from 1928. But it still appears to be standing in a vast open ground in a dilapidated state. A few years back, the Aggarwal community in Delhi took upon the responsibility to maintain this *baoli*. They have set up a small temporary Portakabin in the premise. A guard stays in a small room attached to the north of the mosque, which must have been built for the keeper of the mosque back then.

A remarkable view of the *baoli* with the four storeys. Arches open into the chamber over the tank. The wall separating the well from the tank can also be seen with small openings at the bottom and in the second level.

Dome over the tank, as seen from the basin. It is now the abode of bats.

Location	Hailey Road
Period	Feroz Shah Tughlaq
Public Access	Allowed
Managing Authority	Archaeological Survey of India
Water Level	None
Latitude-Longitude	28.626082, 77.225030
Nearest Metro Station	Barakhamba Road Metro Station
Distance to Nearest Metro Station	1 km (approx.)

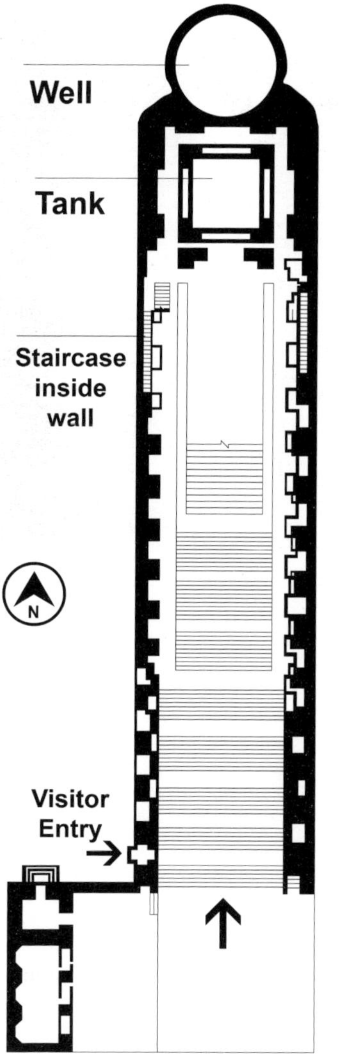

Plan of Ugrasen ki Baoli

MUNIRKA BAOLI

मुनीरका बावली   منیرکا باولی   ਮੁਨੀਰਕਾ ਬਾਓਲੀ

The *baoli* with its two levels and two towers on top. It has staircase to access the platform in the tier below.

Previous page: View from the south-west corner of the first storey of Munirka Baoli. The Wazirpur Gumbad is visible to the north of the *baoli*.

This *baoli* is mentioned as Munirka *Baoli* in a few old records. However, if one tries to explore the present Munirka village, nothing but a dilapidated tomb known as Malik Munirka is spotted. Research on Delhi's heritage requires a deeper knowledge of the localities and how they were reorganized. To find the *baoli* of Munirka, we need to check government land records between 1950 and 1960, when a portion of land near this village was taken to form Rama Krishna Puram (popularly known as R.K. Puram). The *baoli* of Munirka today falls in Sector 5 of this new locality and is part of a Lodhi-era complex, which comprises of five tombs, a prayer wall (Qanati Masjid), few grave platforms, and a stepwell. This complex, documented as Wazirpur Gumbad Complex, stands gracefully between a modern-day gurdwara and a temple, giving the perfect example of communal coexistence.

The most striking element of this *baoli* is its design. Two turrets at the southern end stand on the edge of the well, with narrow winding staircase. They act as alternate approaches to the platform, which divides the *baoli* from the well. The platform has four approaches, two from the turrets and two towards

The platform that separates the well from the tank. An arch in the middle opens towards the well on the left, while another one opposite it opens towards the tank on the right.

View of the well and turrets, with the aqueduct connected to the wall of the well

the sidewalls of the *baoli*, which merge into the staircase midway. The platform has also two arches in the middle, opposite to each other. One opens towards the well, and the other towards the tank. The *baoli* has only two tiers and was filled with earth till the early twentieth century. Measuring 100 feet by 38 feet with a 14 feet circular well to the south, this is one of the smaller *baoli*s of Delhi (along with Dwarka Baoli and the Baoli of Arab ki Sarai). The upper tier contains recessed arches throughout the wall, and the lower level is plain. Towards the south, on the lower level, we have a huge arch that connects the well and the tank. The tank also has a tiny circular well, which has small winding steps along the circular wall. At the top edge of the well, there is an open aqueduct. It has a slope that can help water run down a few feet. The material and the style of the aqueduct suggest that it was built much later for the convenience of the villagers. They would put their vessels at the end of this elevated watercourse, and someone would continuously pour water into the duct. Ladies would queue up at this end, which made it easier and organized to fetch water for daily chores. The main populated area of Munirka village is at a distance. Women would have to walk a lot to fetch water. Due to the absence of any other reference to a waterbody in the vicinity, one can assume that this was the major source of water, besides the Neela Hauz, which is further than this *baoli*. There is also a possibility that some dwellings came up around this structure, which must have been relocated when R.K. Puram was being planned.

This monument complex is under ASI and is now well-maintained. Locals practice yoga in the morning and evening on its well-manicured lawns. Since 2016, some locals have started offering flowers and sweets

A small well-like structure under the tank with a winding staircase. The wall has the lower arch sealed, which would have been the access between the tank and the well. The upper arches are on the platform above.

at the graves in the main tomb in this complex. Since the burial tombs are of unknown people, local devotees have given them the title of 'Pir Baba'. They also sometimes ask visitors to remove their shoes before entering the tomb.

Interestingly, to the east of this *baoli* is a well, which was probably built later. The question one may ask here: if the *baoli* with a well was already there, what was the need for a separate well? Two theories strike my mind. One, probably the *baoli* was all dried up by then, and digging the *baoli*-well deeper was not feasible. So, they had to construct a separate well, deeper than the *baoli*. Two, it could be that the well was constructed for a different community/caste, as was the practice back then. But if it was for a different caste, chances are that it should have been further away from this *baoli*. So the first theory sounds more believable here.

To reach this *baoli*, one may simply ask for Sector 5 gurdwara in R.K. Puram. As you turn to Vivekananda Marg from Palam Marg, the first (gated) entry to your left takes you inside Sector 5. Behind the gate, you encounter a huge park. The tomb complex is right behind this park.

Steps of the *baoli*, along with the Wazirpur Gumbad, visible from the arch opening towards the tank on the platform

The turrets and the well with tombs visible at the back

Right: Plan of the Munirka Baoli

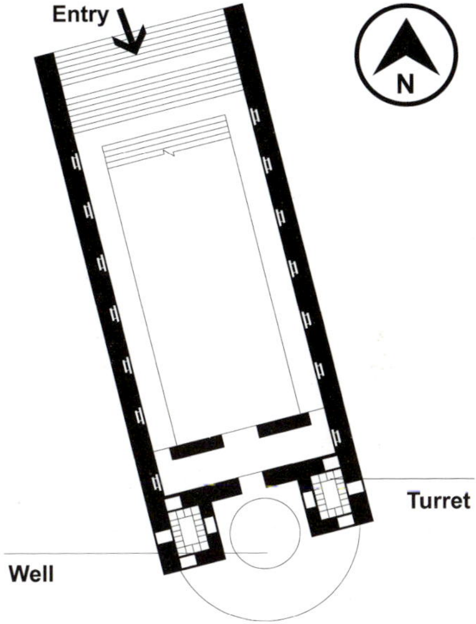

Location	Wazirpur Gumbad Complex, Sector 5, R.K. Puram
Period	Lodhi
Public Access	Allowed
Managing Authority	Archaeological Survey of India
Water Level	Dry
Latitude-Longitude	28.562246, 77.175029
Nearest Metro Station	Munirka Metro Station
Distance to Nearest Metro Station	800 metres (approx.)

GANDHAK KI BAOLI

गंधक की बावली　گندھک کی باولی　ਗੰਧਕ ਦੀ ਬਾਓਲੀ

A commanding view of Gandhak ki Baoli, with kids preparing to take a dip in the tank

Previous page: Gandhak ki Baoli seen in the shape of a huge five-tiered structure. The local boys are seen to take a bath in the tank.

As the story goes, Sultan Shams-ud-Din Iltutmish (aka Altamash) visited Khwaja Qutb-ud-Din Bakhtiyar Kaki, the famous Sufi mystic of Mehrauli. Khwaja Kaki was the immediate successor of Khwaja Moinuddin Chishti of Ajmer, and was treated as his master by the sultan. Upon his unannounced arrival, the sultan found that the saint was in a dishevelled and untidy state. He was informed that due to lack of potable water, the residents of this *khanqah* (residence/monastery), including the saint himself, were forced to stay in such a shape and save water for necessary routines. Hearing this, the emperor immediately commissioned a stepwell on the eastern side of the village, which now serves as the entry of Khwaja Kaki's dargah. This was the very first stepwell in Delhi. Prior to this, we only had wells and stepped ponds like Anangtal (Sanjay Van, Mehrauli) and Surajkund (Faridabad).

As the folklore suggests, Iltutmish held himself responsible, as Khwaja Kaki had migrated to Mehrauli on his request some time back. Now the saint had to live in a miserable state because of the lack of resources. We do not have a definite evidence of whether he had already commissioned Hauz-i-Shamsi on the other side of the village by this time, but even if he had, it was too far for Khwaja Kaki to ensure an adequate supply of water round the clock. As Iltutmish commissioned the new *baoli* near the dargah, he also ensured that it got completed as soon as possible. As a result, no attention was paid to the ornamentation or even building rooms in its walls. There is also a possibility that since this was the first attempt of its kind in the city, masons and architects did not think of any ornamentation. As the masons reached the aquifer, they realized that they had pierced the rock which was rich in sulphate. This rock runs till Sohna (near Gurgaon), as we have a hot spring there inside the Shiva temple. Sulphur mixes well with water and, if available in the right quantity, it turns water into medicine. Water with sulphur traces is good for the skin and hair. It can cure acne, hay fever, rosacea, dandruff, scaly skin, lice, cold sores, and infections caused by poison oak or ivy. It may have laxative effects if consumed for drinking in large quantity, but it is still very good for bathing. The people of Mehrauli took it as a miracle and named this *baoli* 'Gandhak ki Baoli' (the stepwell of sulphur). Almost every traveller or historian who visited this *baoli* has written that kids jump into this *baoli* from the upper levels for the amusement of visitors and,

A picture of Gandhak ki Baoli caught in the lens in 2010. All the five levels are clearly visible, and very less water can be spotted in the tank.

Picture taken from the edge of the well, with the aqueduct visible on the left and the *baoli* filled with mossy water

The well of the *baoli* with stones projected on the top, which used to hold the wooden structure that contained the pulley or the Persian Wheel to fetch water from the well hence, the *baoli* has received its English nickname—'The Diving Well'. The tradition is continued till date.

Gandhak ki Baoli is situated on Dargah Road in Mehrauli. As you enter the village from Adham Khan's tomb or Mehrauli Bus Terminal, turn left on to Dargah Road. At the corner of the road, which turns towards Mehrauli post office, you will find a cluster of shacks selling junk jewellery, tea, and accessories used by fakirs. Hidden behind these stores is the tiny entrance to Mehrauli's deepest *baoli*. Till a few years back, the *baoli* was completely dry. Some restoration work and desilting helped the water to return. This rubble masonry *baoli* measures 133 feet by 34 feet 9 inches and is five storeys deep. Each level is smaller in size than the one above it. This allows pathways on the east and west sides, leading to the corridor on the south that separates the water tank and the well. The five-storeyed corridors to the south are made of stone pillars.

An old picture suggests that there used to be a *hauz* (tank) right at the entrance of the *baoli* in the north-west. It was less than one-fourth the length of the *baoli* and a few feet wide. This tank is right behind the entry gate and is now filled with concrete. Due to a lack of documentation about this tank, the exact

A snapshot taken in 2010, showing steps leading down to the tank when the *baoli* had no water

usage cannot be determined. However, upon close observation, one can see an aqueduct running along a wall of the *baoli* from the edge of the well to this tank. It seems rather obvious that the tank provided water to people visiting the dargah of Khwaja Qutb-ud-Din Bakhtiyar Kaki. It might not have been easy to walk down this deep stepwell for water. Also, the dargah has always been an important site of pilgrimage, visited by thousands of devotees each year. The *baoli* is not wide enough to accommodate the crowd. Such a tank would have been a very important element. Someone at the well would pour water into this aqueduct and fill the tank, from where large gathering of devotees could easily fetch water.

Though the water today is not very clean, kids still spend their summer afternoons in the tank by taking dives. A century back, when the water was clean, regular diving competitions were organized at this *baoli* and people from all across the country would come here to show their talent.

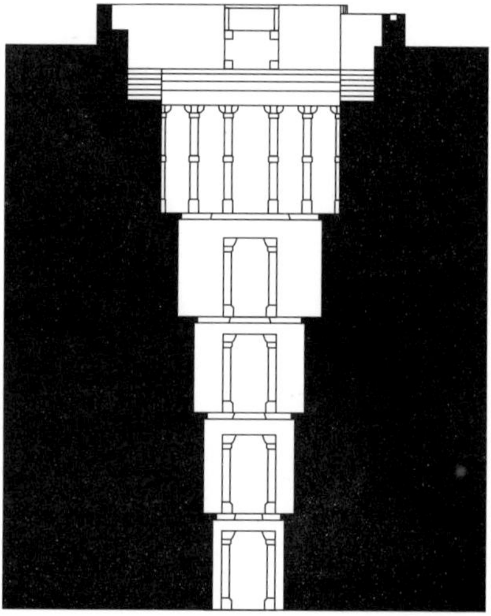

Drawing of the front section of the Gandhak ki Baoli that connects the well and the tank

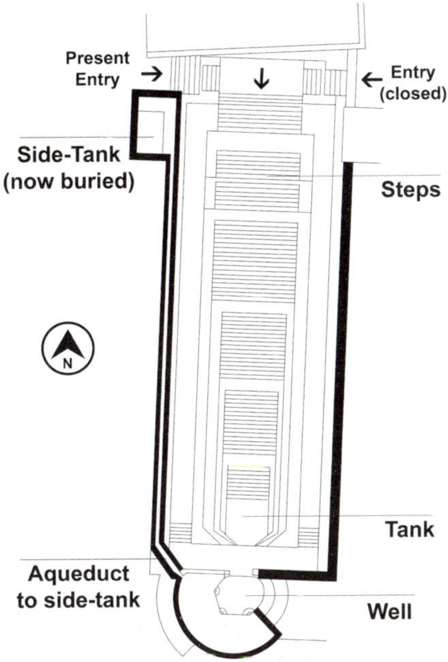

Plan of Gandhak ki Baoli

Location	At the entry road to the dargah
Period	Iltutmish
Public Access	Allowed
Managing Authority	Archaeological Survey of India
Water Level	Filled with unclean water
Latitude-Longitude	28.520869, 77.181603
Nearest Metro Station	Qutub Minar Metro Station
Distance to Nearest Metro Station	2 kms (approx.)

PURANA QILA BAOLI

पुराने किले की बावली   پرانے قلعے کی باولی   ਪੁਰਾਣੇ ਕਿਲੇ ਦੀ ਬਾਓਲੀ

Surprisingly, all historic records are silent on this *baoli*. To find information about this *baoli*, one needs to find records related to the village of Indarpat that existed inside the Purana Qila (Old Fort) nearly a century ago. When the capital was transferred to Delhi from Calcutta in 1912, the relocation of 1,900 inhabitants of the Indarpat village became a challenge. The southern half of the citadel (Old Fort) was occupied by people, who were then relocated to Rohtak, Bulandshahr, and Gurgaon, amongst few other areas. A total of Rs. 1,44,183 was paid at that time as compensation. When the homes were removed around Sher Mandal, British engineers found a pit filled with mud and garbage. Upon clearing, the large dump turned out to be a deep *baoli*.

When the *baoli* was fully restored, it had eighty-nine steps, covering a depth of 73 feet to reach the water level. The flight of steps has eight landings, the position of which is marked by means of recessed

Facing page: A set of steps going down towards the tank. The lower end of the structure is engulfed in darkness and the walls overgrown with algae and moss.

niches in the side walls. Unlike most other *baoli*s in Delhi, this one has its well towards the north-east, which communicates with the tank through a standard window at the base. The tank is covered with a roof and the *baoli* has no chambers or levels above the tank. We only have few arches in the wall, closer to the tank, which may have been used to store things like buckets. It also has few simple alcoves near the tank, which were probably used to keep lamps to light the bottom of the *baoli*. This is perhaps one of the simplest *baoli*s that we have in Delhi.

Left to right: A narrow flight of eighty-nine steps, separated by eight landings and descending to a depth of twenty-two metres, gives access to the groundwater

Small arches to keep items and alcoves to hold lamps near the tank along both walls of the *baoli*

Arches visible on the sidewalls near the tank. The main platform over the tank is strengthened by a sturdy vault.

This *baoli* does not have any inscription, but the south gate of Old Fort had a well-formed Naskh inscription on the western pier of the northern arch of the upper storey. This inscription was not carved but written with a standard black ink, which faded away with

A modern room constructed to cover the well and to protect the machinery that pumps water out of the well for irrigation

time. Maulvi Zafar Hasan was able to record it and provided its translation as follows:

The gate of the peaceful valley was completed in the reign of Sher Shah who wears a crown.
By order of Ghazi Khan Lohani who is a loyal well-wisher of the king.
The king has spent an abundance of silver and gold (on the construction) so that there may remain a memorial to him through the years.
It was in the year 950 resplendent made bright.

From the given inscription, we can ascertain the date and construction of this *baoli*, which appears to be of the same period as the gate.

Today, the well is covered with a room that has a motorized pump which pulls water out of this *baoli* and irrigates the well-manicured lawns of the Purana Qila.

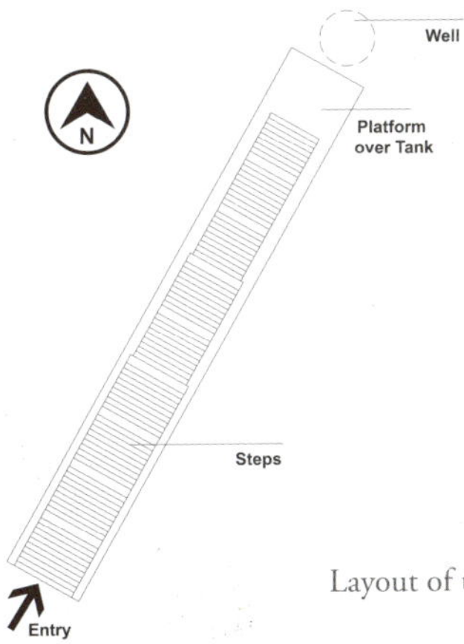

Layout of the Old Fort Baoli

Location	Inside Purana Qila (Old Fort)
Period	Sher Shah Suri
Public Access	Allowed
Managing Authority	Archaeological Survey of India
Water Level	Very low
Latitude-Longitude	28.609377, 77.244378
Nearest Metro Station	Khan Market Metro Station
Distance to Nearest Metro Station	1.4 kms (approx.)

RAJON KI BAOLI

राजों की बैन راجون کی باین ਰਾਜੇਯਾਂ ਦੀ ਬਾਓਲੀ

Hiding in plain sight—a picture of the ornamental stepwell from 2017, with three levels visible

Previous page: A picturesque view of Rajon ki Baoli with numerous arched recesses that provided rest to visitors

Deep inside the Mehrauli Archaeological Park stands Rajon ki Baoli (or Rajon ki Bain). Unlike other *baoli*s in Delhi, the exterior of this one is beautifully decorated. However, since the access is from the north side, hardly anyone gets a glance at the beautiful stucco work behind the well towards the south. Few photographs from the nineteenth century show the decorated arches around the well. They appear closed in photographs from the twentieth century. This oblong-shaped *baoli* was built during the reign of Sikandar Shah Lodhi. Sir Syed Ahmad Khan attributes Daulat Khan as the builder of this *baoli*.

Daulat Khan was the governor of Jalandhar in Punjab with Sultanpur Lodhi as his capital. This is the same Sultanpur where the founder of Sikhism, Guru Nanak, was employed as a keeper of the granaries of Daulat Khan. Later, Khan was given charge of entire Punjab and moved his capital to Lahore. It is said that Daulat Khan played an important role in the power struggle between his sovereign Sultan Ibrahim Lodhi and his relatives. He was favouring Sultan's uncle Alam Khan. Daulat Khan's sons brought news from Delhi that Sultan Ibrahim was planning to remove him from governorship. This enraged Daulat Khan and he invited Babur to India. The rest is history.

As you read about Daulat Khan, you realize that he was a very influential personality whose fame spread far and wide, from Delhi to Gujarat and Punjab. He must have commissioned numerous buildings across his region. Rajon ki Baoli is the most ornate *baoli* in Mehrauli and resonates with Daulat Khan's stature.

The *baoli* is four storeys deep with a well towards the south. The top two storeys are surrounded by an

A picture from 2011, with all the four storeys visible and little water present in the tank. The arched halls on all the three sides are cool, shaded, and have floral patterns on the medallions on the exterior that survive only on one side.

arcade with massive piers. Three arches on the inner southern side of the top storey are sealed, with stairs on both sides to reach the roof. Behind these stairs is a hidden slit in the wall that takes you to the second level, and a corridor with stone pillars and arch openings into the deep well. There are big boulders penetrating out of the eastern wall and leaning into the *baoli* tank. Normally, the area is cleared well before constructing something. However, in this case, these huge rocks were left intact with two storeys built beneath and two above them. Each level has small alcoves built, perhaps, for the earthen lamps. One can visualize the beauty of the *baoli*, with all four storeys well-lit and the light from the moon reflecting in the tank. The plaster on the inner western side of the top storey was damaged at some point in history. During the recent restoration, the wall was covered with plain plaster. However, one can imagine the beauty of the entire *baoli* by looking at the beautiful stucco medallions on the east.

There is a mosque attached to the *baoli* towards the west. The mosque has a beautiful entrance from the south, which is now sealed by the authorities for security reasons. The only way to get inside the mosque is by a small staircase leading to the roof of

The western wall of the *baoli* with a mosque and a tomb visible on the upper level

Twelve-pillared tomb in the courtyard of the mosque

the arches around the *baoli*, from where visitors climb over into the mosque's courtyard through a small opening in the wall. This three-chambered mosque is beautifully decorated with plaster from the inside, and on the exterior, the medallions around the arches bear the name of God. The medallion outside the central arch has a verse of Quran written on it.

The courtyard of the mosque has a tomb, built with twelve stone pillars and a dome resting on them.

The interior of the dome and the drum of the tomb

The drum under this dome was once decorated with blue tiles, traces of which can still be seen. The red sandstone plaque on the southern side of this drum mentions a few names. Carr Stephen, a British officer, gives its translation as:

> In the reign of gracious [King], [a] king greater than then great [kings], with faith in the merciful: Sikandar Shah, son of Bahlul Shah Sultan, may God perpetuate his reign and his kingdom; [this pavilion was] built by the slave, who hopes for the mercy of the protector, Khan Daulat, son of Khwaja Muhammad, on the first of the month of Rajab, in the year 922 [Hijri].

The inside of the drum is incised with floral patterns and Qur'anic verses.

Bashir-ud-Din Ahmad, in his monumental work *Waqiaat-e-Darul Hukumat Delhi*, talks about some of the rooms in this *baoli*. He also mentions that people are using the attached mosque as their kitchen, and that black smoke from their clay ovens has turned the ceiling of the mosque pitch-black. Sir Syed Ahmad Khan also speaks of the rooms and even provides an illustration of the *baoli* in which the top row of the arches is covered with bricks, leaving a door in each. There is a probability that the arches were covered

Interior of the mosque with blackened ceiling and scribbles in Persian

A picture from 1908 showing foliage around the dilapidated and dried *baoli. Source: ASI Photo Archives*

A 1923 picture of the steps of the *baoli*, tomb, and the mosque with Adham Khan's tomb visible at a distance. Other buildings around Adham Khan's tomb no longer exist. *Source: ASI Photo Archives*

A 1919 picture showing the dilapidated *baoli* and tank filled with earth. The fourth storey is buried and was revealed decades later. *Source: ASI Photo Archives*

up to be converted into rooms and were being used by people. Almost every author and historian has mentioned about masons staying in these rooms. Locally, the masons are called *raje* or *raaj-mistry*. Clearly, this is where the *baoli* gets its name from.

The *baoli* dried up long back and earned a new name—'Sookhi Baoli'. However, the desilting process carried out by the ASI resulted in the return of water, and the *baoli* is now filled up to two levels.

An arresting view of the *baoli* steps and tank through an archway of the second storey

View of the well from bottom-up. Extruded stones with holes were fitted with wooden frame containing the pulley or the Persian Wheel to draw water.

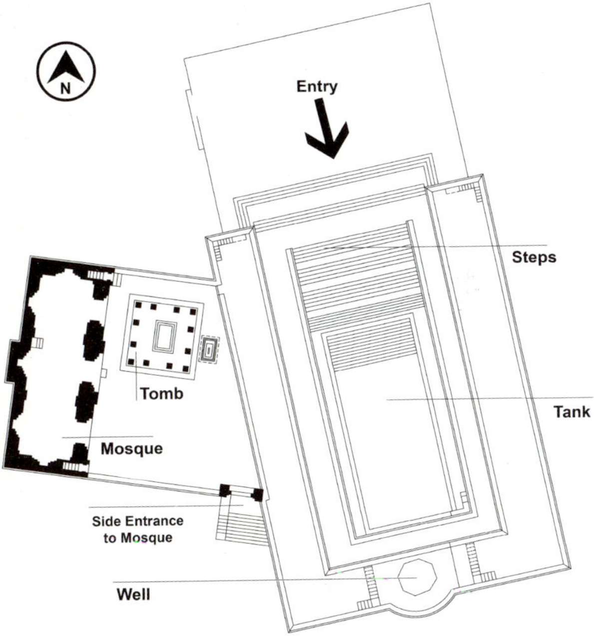

Plan of Rajon ki Baoli

Location	Mehrauli Archaeological Park
Period	Sikandar Lodhi
Public Access	Allowed
Managing Authority	Archaeological Survey of India
Water Level	Filled with unclean water
Latitude–Longitude	28.520530, 77.183454
Nearest Metro Station	Qutub Minar Metro Station
Distance to Nearest Metro Station	1.5 kms (approx.)

LOHARHERI BAOLI

लोहारहेड़ी की बावली

لوہارہڑی کی باولی

ਲੋਹਾਰਹੇੜੀ ਦੀ ਬਾਉਲੀ

The *baoli* in a dilapidated and neglected state, used as a garbage dump. Picture taken in 2012.

Previous page: The Loharheri Baoli, a structure exemplary of Lodhi-era architecture, with arches along the steps and a well at the end of the *baoli*. The two levels of arches are clearly visible along the steps.

In 2011, one report in a newspaper took many Delhiites by surprise. It spoke of a *baoli* in Dwarka, and soon after this report, agencies got active to restore it. Before 2011, the *baoli* was not visible clearly. One could only see the outer rim of the well, with a small portion of the shaft visible. The tank was nothing but a deep pit with a mud ramp reaching it. It was covered with dense vegetation, and locating it was a challenging task.

A couple of years after the news broke, Indian National Trust for Art and Cultural Heritage (INTACH) started restoring the structure, and upon cleaning, the steps, walls, and the well were completely revealed. The trees and the untended vegetation were removed, a protective wall was created around it, and a Portakabin placed for the guard.

Old records reveal this *baoli* to be in a village called Loharheri. The name suggests that it might have been a settlement of ironsmiths. Maulvi Zafar Hasan's listing of Delhi's monuments talk of this *baoli* and mentions of another *baoli* in the vicinity, which has not been found yet. The other one is the *baoli* of Teghanpur village, three-fourth mile east to the village of Amberhai, as mentioned in his records. It should be around Sector 9 in Dwarka. The Loharheri Baoli is the smallest *baoli* in Delhi, with a size of 52 feet by 16 feet 6 inches. It has just twenty-two steps leading to the tank. It is attached to the wall of Gangotri Apartments in Sector 12, Dwarka, on Azad Hind Fauj Marg. The *baoli* appears to be a close replica of the Wazirpur Baoli in R.K. Puram, except for the turrets at the end. Like the Munirka Baoli, this one also has small winding steps inside the small, well-like pit at the base of the tank. Like most other *baolis*, its main well is towards the south with steps leading from the north to the south of the tank.

Location	Azad Hind Fauj Marg, Sector 12, Dwarka
Period	Sikandar Lodhi
Public Access	Allowed
Managing Authority	Govt. of Delhi
Water Level	None
Latitude-Longitude	28.599791, 77.044067
Nearest Metro Station	Dwarka Sector 12 & 13 Metro Stations
Distance to Nearest Metro Station	1.7 kms (approx.)

The walls of the three-storeyed *baoli*, with openings in the back wall connecting the well to the tank. The side walls have two sets of recessed arches.

A set of steps leading down to the tank

The *baoli* shares wall with the Gangotri Apartment in Dwarka, Sector 12

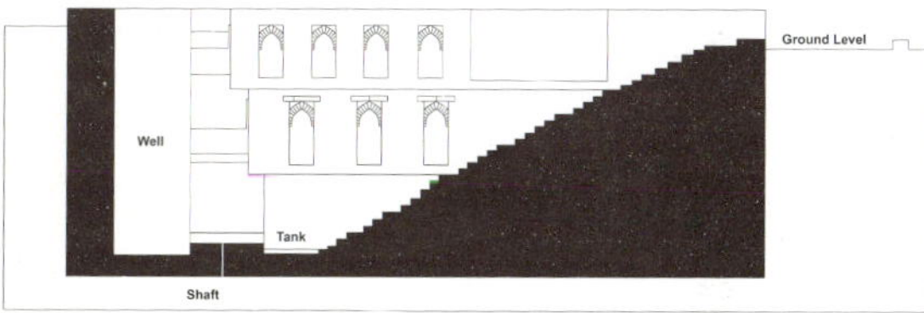

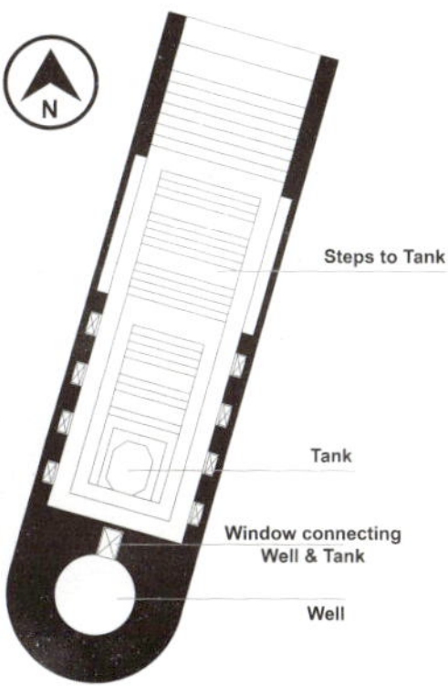

Top: Section drawing of Loharheri Baoli

Left: Plan of Loharheri Baoli

BAOLI OF MEHERBAN AGHA'S MANDI— ARAB KI SARAI

अरब सराए की बावली عرب سرا کی باولی ਅਰਬ ਸਰਾਇ ਦੀ ਬਾਓਲੀ

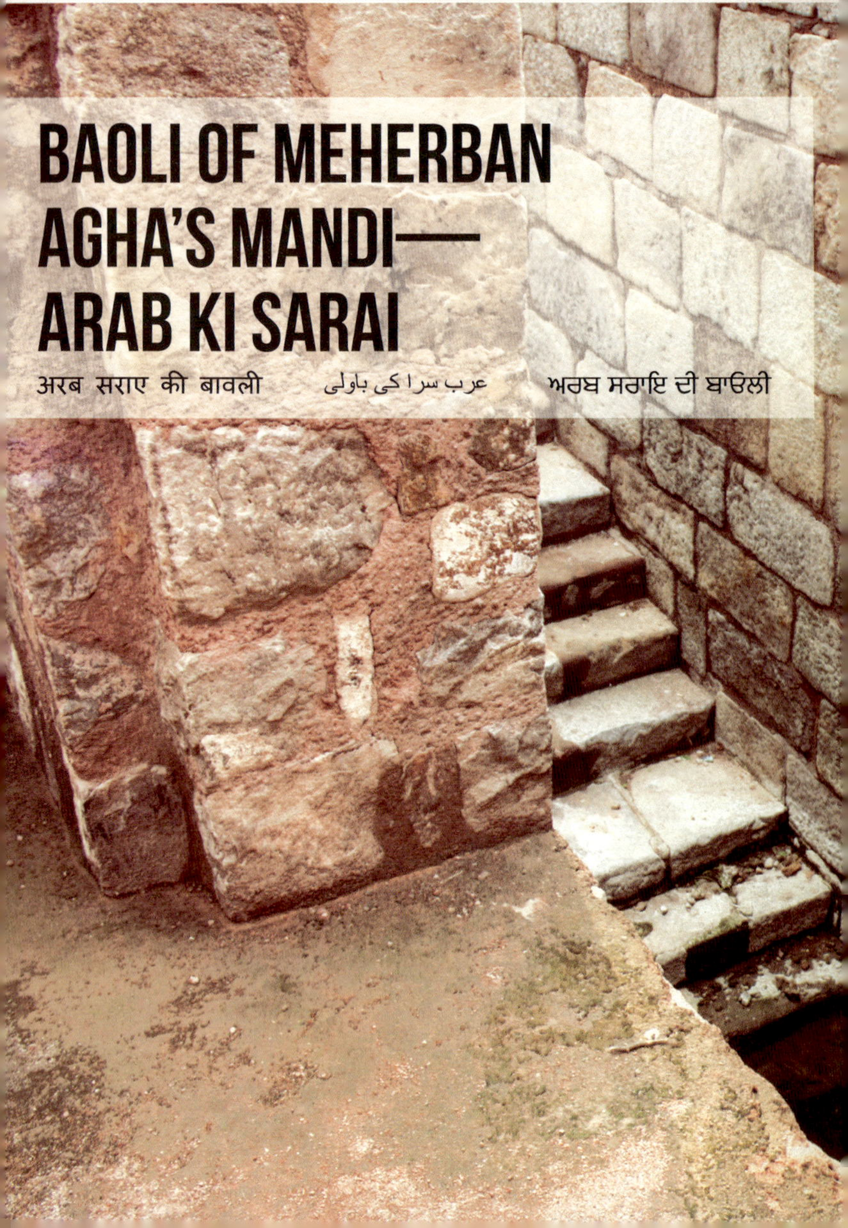

Arched entrance leading to the platform above the tank

Previous page: Stone steps leading to the tank

It will be an injustice to exclude this *baoli* from the list. It has existed as yet another forgotten structure in one corner of the world-famous Humayun's Tomb complex.

As the story goes, the wife of Emperor Humayun, Hamida Banu Begum, brought 300 Arabs from her pilgrimage to Mecca and settled them in Delhi. She built a caravanserai for them, now popular by the name 'Arab ki Sarai'. The serai is sandwiched between Isa Khan's Tomb and Humayun's tomb enclosure, inside the World Heritage Site of Humayun's tomb complex. Its main entry gate is towards north, adjoining the gate of the garden of Bu Halima, another monument within the complex. Only a mosque and a tomb, known as Afsarwala, survive today inside this serai. However, to the south of this serai, a fruit and vegetable market was built during the reign of Emperor Jahangir, by a eunuch named Meherban Agha. His name is mentioned as Meherban Agha by Sir Syed Ahmed Khan and Bashir-ud-Din Ahmed in their Urdu works. However, Maulvi Zafar, in his English listing, spells him as Mihr Banu. Later, English works picked up the spellings of Zafar Hasan. The south gate of Arab ki Sarai was used as the entry gate to this *mandi* (market). There are several arcaded chambers that functioned as shops, but what excites most is that it has two wells very close to each other. One of the well has steps leading to the tank, thus making it a *baoli*. Bashir-ud-Bin Ahmad, in his book *Waqiaat-e-Darul Hukumat Delhi* (1919), mentions that this stepwell was connected to a mosque, which is now gone. Sir Syed Ahmed Khan in his *Asar-us-Sanadid* also mentions this

Remains of the arches that once strengthened the platform above them

market, the mosque, and the stepped well under it. Both Sir Syed and Bashir-ud-Din mention that the locals call it *bain* (another name for *baoli*). Most other historians have not taken note of this stepwell inside the complex.

The stepwell of Arab ki Sarai has its own unique architecture. The well is towards the south and a tank is extended to the north. Steps lead to a platform above the tank from north to south. This platform

The circular structure of the *baoli* well

The eastern arch of the tank, as seen from the platform above it

gives access to the well. A separate twenty-metre-long flight of steps descends from the west to the east, reaching the tank. It is a very small structure, measuring approximately 90 feet by 46 feet. This makes it the second smallest *baoli* after the Loharheri Baoli of Dwarka. There are no rooms/chambers within the *baoli*. However, the strong arches show that this was an underground structure, and a building (a mosque, as suggested by Sir Syed and Bashir-ud-Din Ahmad) must have been on top of it. The roof, however, is now gone. Being part of the UNESCO World Heritage Complex, this *baoli* is well kept and has water, which is not being used currently.

Location	Inside Meherban's Mandi, Arab ki Sarai
Period	Jahangir
Public Access	Allowed (with permission)
Managing Authority	Archaeological Survey of India
Water Level	Filled with water
Latitude-Longitude	28.591081, 77.248253
Nearest Metro Station	JLN Stadium Metro Station
Distance to Nearest Metro Station	2 kms (approx.)

BAOLI OF DARGAH KHWAJA KAKI (HAFIZ DAWOOD KI BAOLI)

दरगाह काकी की बावली　درگاہ حضرت کاکی کی باولی　ਦਰਗਾਹ ਕਾਕੀ ਦੀ ਬਾਓਲੀ

The arch that appeared after desilting. Water returned to the tank when further cleaning was done.

Previous page: The hall, built by Dawood, with huge colonial columns and girders with roof slabs

While the *baoli* inside the dargah of Khwaja Qutb-ud-Din Bakhtiyar Kaki in Mehrauli did not make it to the list of top ten, the book will be incomplete without its mention. This *baoli* exists within the complex of the dargah, completely hidden from the outside world. It is not as old as the dargah or any other *baoli* in or around Delhi. However, it still holds an important place in history. The *baoli* of Hazrat Kaki's dargah is one of those well-documented structures which were neglected with time. I met Fauzan Sahab, the manager of the dargah, during an event in the Delhi University, where we both were panelists discussing the water situation in Delhi. Impressed by one of my responses, he invited me to visit the *baoli*. The following week, I was there with a few friends, exploring the Zafar Mahal and nearby structures, when I bumped into Fauzan Sahab and he took us all to his office. During a round of tea, he told us how he has been pushing the local authorities to do something about this *baoli*. He mentioned that the government sent a team to clean the *baoli* some time back. However, the contractor did not complete his job. He stopped after cleaning sixty feet, instead of eighty feet, as instructed

Area under the hall which shows the *baoli* to be in a very bad condition. Picture clicked in October 2018.

by the government officials. It was only after the hard pushing of Mr Fauzan that he agreed to desilt the *baoli* twenty feet further. As they were about to stop, water appeared and the *baoli* was immediately filled with clean groundwater. It is estimated that this *baoli* has forty to fifty feet of water filling the tank. There is a large hall which was built to provide additional space for visitors, but was hardly used. The well of the *baoli* is uncovered and exploited as a garbage bin by a few houses that surround the well. The roof of the *baoli*,

Portion of the well/tank that is open. It is enclosed by houses on three sides and used by people as garbage bin.

which also acts as the courtyard of the dargah and bears the load of thousands of devotees each day, has started showing signs of wear and tear. While some measures have been taken to prevent a mishap, better remedies are required to prevent complete caving in of the concrete structure.

While all other *baoli*s in Delhi date back to the Tughlaqs and Lodhis, this was built just a decade before the British took over completely. What amuses

Steps going down to the lower level of the *baoli*. The original wooden door is visible at the edge of the steps.

me more is that the area of Mehrauli was densely populated, and still a man managed space to build this huge structure.

In 1844, a noble named Hafiz Muhammad Dawood Khan Mustaqeem Jung felt that the demand for water by the visitors of the dargah was not being adequately met. Water was sourced from the distant *baoli*s or wells. He, therefore, decided to build one *baoli* connected to the dargah. Construction started in 1844 and was completed in the year 1845 at a cost of Rs. 14,000 at that time. He copied the design of Hazrat Nizam-ud-Din's *baoli* to construct this structure. Hafiz Dawood came from a well-respected family, tracing his roots to Hazrat Imam Abu Hanifa, the founder of Sunni Hanafi School of fiqh (Islamic jurisprudence).

Seal on the metal girder bearing the year 1898 that hints at some restoration work carried out earlier

Over the steps of the *baoli*, Dawood built a large audience hall. The roof of this audience hall is now the courtyard between Majlis Khana and the dargah mosque. Entrance to the *baoli* is through a narrow winding staircase hidden behind a few graves towards the west of the courtyard. The hall was perhaps repaired some time later, as the metal girders used in it bear the seal reading 'P & W MACLELLAN CLUTHA WORKS LIMITED, GLASGOW, 1898'. The same company was employed to construct and repair several other structures in India. The famous Chenab Bridge was an engineering marvel of that time, also built by this company.

Location	Inside Dargah Hz. Kaki, Mehrauli
Period	Late Mughal
Public Access	Allowed (with permission)
Managing Authority	Dargah Management
Water Level	Filled with unclean water
Latitude-Longitude	28.519045, 77.180885
Nearest Metro Station	Qutub Minar Metro Station
Distance to Nearest Metro Station	2 kms (approx.)

Acknowledgements

While this book focusses on *baolis*, the journey to put it to shape took several turns. I have learned from almost everyone I met, and the journey continues. My father S. Gurdev Singh played an important role in developing this interest of history in me. But it was just limited to evening tea discussions and sharing stories until I decided to explore Delhi with my friend Gaurav Pandey. He has always been enthusiastic about experiments and explorations. When I proposed the idea of exploring Delhi, he was the first one to step forward. It was also due to the encouragement of dear friends Gaurav and Abhishek Dangwal that my research on Delhi's heritage started taking shape. I switched from studying about Delhi to clicking photographs of Delhi with my brother Arvinder. My exploration took a major leap after I met Shri K.K. Muhammed, then superintending archaeologist of Delhi Circle, ASI. He not only encouraged me to explore more, but also equipped me with all necessary permissions. He also introduced me to Sohail Hashmi, who guided me through my journey and helped me explore some of the *baolis* mentioned in this book. I will always fall short of words when thanking Sohail Sir, for he not only reviewed every line in this book, but also took out time from his busy schedule for the many discussions that we had about the stories and the explanations I have given in this book. Dr Narayani Gupta, Shri Ratish Nanda, Shri Janhwij Sharma, Arjun Kumar, and Priyank Gupta are a few learned souls who always help me recharge my thoughts and explore more.

In this journey of exploring our heritage, my dear friend Tauseef Ahmed stood continuously with me and was always ready to support every cause I introduced.

My supervisor Mr Praveen Rao pushed me to never leave my passion and keep working on what I love. His guidance gave me new energy, and my passion became my obsession.

My gratefulness to Niyogi Books who worked painstakingly to convert my writings into a more presentable manner.

Nupur Bhatnagar deserves a special mention for her contribution of all the illustrations and drawings in the book. She also helped me find and verify the facts at the National Archives and Libraries. Without her, this book may not have been as well presented as it is now.

At the final stage of this book, it was Shuv and Tripti who pulled me out of my house to roam around and click better pictures.

Finally, I would like to thank my wife Maninder for her support and encouragement in this journey.

References

Ahmad, Bashir-ud-Din. 1919. *Waqiaat-e-Darul Hukumat Delhi*. Delhi.

Archaeological Survey of India. 2004. *Inventory of Monuments and Sites of National Importance, Delhi Circle*. New Delhi: The Director General of the Archaeological Survey of India.

Cole, Henry Hardy. 1872. *The Architecture of Ancient Delhi: Especially the Buildings Around the Kutb Minar*. London: Arundel Society.

Cooper, Frederick. 1865. *The Handbook for Delhi*. Lahore: T.C. McCarthly.

Cunningham, Alexander, J.D. Beglar, and A.C.L. Carlleyle. 1874. *Archaeology Survey of India: Report for the Year 1871–72: Delhi [and] Agra*. Office of the Superintendent of Government Printing.

Elliot, H.M. and J. Dawson. 2006 [1867]. Zia-ud Din Barni, Shams-i Siraj 'Afif, *Tarikh-i Firoz Shahi*. Lahore: Sang-e Meel Publications.

Fanshaw, H.C. 1902. *Delhi Past and Present*. London: J. Murray.

Guerrieri, Pilar Maria. 2017. *Maps of Delhi*. Delhi: Niyogi Books.

Harcourt, Alfred Frederick Pollock. 1866. *The New Guide to Delhi*. Allahabad: G.A. Savielle.

Hasan, Maulvi Zafar. 1916. *Monuments of Delhi: Lasting Splendour of the Great Mughals and Others*. New Delhi: Aryan Books International.

Hasan, Maulvi Zafar. 1922. *A Guide to Nizamuddin, Memoir No. 10 of ASI*. Calcutta.

Hearn, Gordon Risley. 1906. *The Seven Cities of Delhi*. London: W. Thacker & Co.

Keene, Henry George. 1882. *A Handbook for Visitors to Delhi and its Neighbourhood*. Calcutta: Thacker, Spink & Co.

Khan, Syed Ahmed. 2003. *Asar-ul Sanadid*. New Delhi: Urdu Academy.

Khawaja, G.S. 2012. *Islamic Architecture of Delhi*. Delhi: Bharatiya Kala Prakashan.

Mani, B.R. 1997. *Delhi: Threshold of the Orient*. Delhi: Aryan Books International.

Nanda, Ratish and Narayani Gupta. 1999. *Delhi: The Built Heritage*. INTACH, Delhi Chapter.

Nath, R. 2010. *Monuments of Delhi: Architectural and Historical*. Delhi: Heritage.

Sanderson, Gordon. 1914. *Delhi Fort: A Guide to the Buildings and Gardens*. Delhi: Manager of Publications.

Sharma, Y.D. 1964. *Delhi and its Neighbourhood*. Archaeological Survey of India, Govt. of India.

Sur, Anuradha Dutta. 2014. *Lal Kot to Lal Qila: The Architectural Heritage of Delhi*. Mumbai: ABI Prints & Publishing Company.

The Delhi Almanac and Souvenir for the Year 1850. 1850. Delhi: Delhi Gazette Press.

The Imperial Gazetteer Atlas of India. 1931. Delhi: Low Price Publications. Reproduction of *The Imperial Gazetteer of India*, vol. 26, new revised edn. Oxford: Clarendon Press.

Wheeler, Edmund. 1857. *What Shall We Do at Delhi?* London: Daniel F. Oakey.

Other forthcoming titles by the same author:

DELHI Heritage TOP 10

Forts

Mosques

Monument Complexes